D1536956

Just Like His Father?

A Guide to Overcoming
Your Child's Genetic Connection
to Antisocial Behavior
Addiction & ADHD

Liane J. Leedom, M.D.

The purpose of this book is to provide accurate and authoritative information about the subject matter covered. The author has made every effort to ensure the information is correct and complete. However, neither the publisher nor the author is engaged in rendering professional advice or services to the individual reader. This book is not a substitute for mental health treatment. If you require such advice or treatment, you should seek the services of a competent mental health professional.

Published by Healing Arts Press, LLC, Fairfield, CT
www.healingartspress.us

Copyright © 2006 by Healing Arts Press, LLC
All rights reserved. This book, or parts thereof, may not be reproduced in any form without permission.

Library of Congress Catalog Number 2006921395
ISBN 09778013-0-6
"The Dash" by Linda Ellis, Copyright 1996 Linda Ellis, www.lindaellis.net.
Cover design assistance: Susan A. Katz, *dotmedia inc.*
Cover photography ©Getty Images

Printed in the United States of America
by Morris Publishing
3212 East Highway 30
Kearney, NE 68847
1-800-650-7888

CONTENTS

CONTENTS

CONTENTS

CONTENTS

CHAPTER 1

INTRODUCTION

Disaster Strikes

In spite of many years of education, a career in psychiatry and a passion for science, I married the wrong men. Fortunately, this book is not about choosing a husband. It is about being a parent, as I have also been a single parent under the most difficult of circumstances. I raised two girls alone after my first husband moved out of the country. Then, when I thought that I had finally found a man who would love and cherish us all, disaster struck in my life. After only 16 months of marriage, my second husband proved beyond any doubt that he was not capable of loving and cherishing anyone. I had been duped, conned into a marriage by someone who had only exploitation on his mind.

Since I had a baby with my second husband; three innocent children were victims of my marital disaster. I had done the unthinkable, chosen a husband who could have really hurt my precious children, and caused us all to have to cope with unthinkable stress.

I felt intense fear when I realized what my ex-husband is—a psychopath. A psychopath is a person with the worst form of a disorder psychiatrists call antisocial personality. I was painfully aware of the volumes of scientific data showing that this disorder is both incurable and genetically transmitted. I held my infant son while disturbing thoughts filled my mind. "What if my little boy grows up to be like his father? (It has always been my belief that we are in this world to do good, what if my son lacks the capacity to share that belief?) If this disorder is genetic, is there nothing I can do? How can I help my son and not be responsible for bringing another psychopath into the world?" The concern over what could be was overwhelming. All those years of education and the best training in psychiatry, had not prepared me for this challenge.

With time, and healing, the shock of what happened dissolved, and I became determined to heal our family. I resolved to study the scientific literature to understand what is known about how antisocial personality disorder develops, and to stop at nothing to be the best parent I could be. As I searched the literature for the science behind parenting my **at risk** son, four truths jumped out at me.

1.   Research regarding the development of antisocial personality disorder does provide real insights into how to prevent this disorder, and interestingly, some of these insights also apply to addiction and attention deficit/hyperactivity disorder (ADHD).

2.   It is hard to find specific parenting guidance because of the difficult scientific terminology found in research articles. The literature is full of technical terms ("psycho-babble"). Among the countless and somewhat humorous examples is the use of the term "MRO." What is MRO? Since love is not a precise scientific term, scientists use initials like MRO (mutually responsive orientation) to mean love.

3.   Given that even with my background, I had to work hard to translate the literature; I wondered how a person without such a background was supposed to fend for him/herself.

4.   The American taxpayer has funded much of the very important research into how humans develop. Yet scientists have not reported the findings of this research in a format the public can understand. We all have a right to the information that will help us care for our children.

"We have a mutually responsive orientation and should spend the rest of our lives together!"

This book contains a summary of the literature regarding the development of antisocial personality disorder and addiction. Since many adults with these disorders suffered from ADHD as children, this book will show you how to cope effectively with symptoms of ADHD in your child. Specific parenting guidelines based on scientific studies, are tied to this summary. As a psychiatrist and parent of an **at risk** child, I am acquainted both professionally and personally, with the many issues that exist in families coping with antisocial personality and addiction. Since an understanding of these issues is also critical for good parenting of the **at risk** child, they are discussed in this book. My sincere wish is to provide comfort to other parents who share my life-challenge. There are many of us, and we all want the best for our kids.

Children of Sorrow Children of Hope

When addicts and those with antisocial personality disorder have children, their families face special challenges. Emotional scars inevitably result from a union with an individual with antisocial personality disorder or addiction. A spouse can end up sharing life with an addict when addiction develops over the course of a marriage. In other cases, conning and trickery are involved. For some, the union results from rape, perhaps a date rape. Most of us would not knowingly or willingly have a child with such a person, thus the reality is some children are born after physical (or what feels like psychological) rape. Thankfully, motherly and fatherly love is so strong that it can overcome these scars.

Since children physically resemble their parents, chances are the innocent child will resemble his not so innocent parent. Therefore, anyone raising such a child needs to be aware that this resemblance may cause unconscious reactions to the child. Physical resemblance often goes beyond the obvious, hair color, eye color and facial features. Children have the mannerisms of their parents, even parents they have never met.

When dealing with a reality as painful as one's own child resembling someone who has done great harm, the first response is often denial. Therefore, stop a moment to question how this resemblance could affect your care of your child. It is not only parents who should look within themselves for the answer to this question, any of those in the family who came into contact with the affected parent, could possibly react to the child in a negative way.

Victims of con artists and rapists, and families of addicts may face significant social stigma. Friends and family often blame the victim. "If he /she hadn't used such poor judgment, bad things would never have happened." I have faced this reality only to be left with the conclusion that if I had been a wiser person, then my son would never have been born. What a terrible thought! I love my son and in spite of my concerns, I have great hope for his future.

"My son, you are here to love and to use your talents to make our world a better place."

In addition to having the awesome responsibility for rearing my son, I must learn to live with the many contradictions that are now part of my life. I am challenged to find hope in the midst of ruin and more importantly, to work to make good out of tragedy. **I must have a vision for the beautiful person my son can become with the right loving care.**

What is my vision for my child? Without a vision of possibilities, and goals for the future, dreams cannot be realized. I have to have a vision for my child's life. That vision will change and become more detailed as he grows and shows his own special qualities. Nevertheless, to begin, I hope my child will be a good person who uses his talents to make the world a better place. Then, as he develops and we discover the aptitudes that make him special, the vision becomes increasingly personal and specific.

It is important for all the caregivers of the **at risk** child to share both a common and specific vision for that child. A well-meaning parent or relative may say, "I just want my child to be happy." This will NOT work for the **at risk** child. People with antisocial personality and those with substance abuse disorders pursue their own happiness at the expense of others. Therefore, the minimum needed to prevent such behavior is to deeply instill the idea that life involves much more than the pursuit of ones own happiness.

In the Genes

It was a hot, sunny summer day and the children of the neighborhood all ran to the ice cream truck. A seven-year-old girl bought a Popsicle. To her surprise and disappointment, an eleven-year-old boy, she had never met, took it from the ice cream man. He said, "She's buying for me, I'm her brother." Six years later, the girl met that neighborhood boy in the woods. This time he claimed he only wanted to talk to her. When she let her guard down, he raped her. Within a week of raping the girl, the boy was arrested for stabbing another boy in a fight.

How do scientists determine if the cause of the callous antisocial behavior of this boy is in his genes or related to his presumably poor upbringing? As of the time of this book, there is no specific test to check the cause of antisocial behavior in this boy, however, thanks to behavioral genetics, scientists have learned a great deal about the causes of antisocial behavior in our society. One problem with behavioral genetics is that genes may determine early environment. This is because the same genes that programmed the makeup of our boy also programmed the makeup of his parents. People with antisocial personality traits or addiction usually make terrible parents. They are often neglectful and abusive, and no one is surprised when their children behave badly. Can you see that often genetics determines **both** an individual's traits and his early environment? It is very sad when you think about it; some kids never really have a chance. They get a double whammy– the genes that make them vulnerable also give them unfit parents.

In order to sort out the causes of these behavioral disorders, scientists must get around the problem of genes determining environment. They do this several ways. First, they examine whether a disorder (or traits of a disorder) is more frequently found in the family members of affected individuals than in the general population. In other words, is a person more likely to have the disorder if others in his family have it, even if they have not shared the same environment? Surveys can also examine whether sets of similar disorders run in extended families. Then, scientists look to see if more closely related individuals within the same family are more likely to have the disorder. Are those who share more genes with an affected person more at risk than less closely related individuals who shared the same environment? Identical twins share 100 per cent of the same genes. Children share about 50 per cent of each parent's genes. Non-identical twins are just like siblings when it comes to sharing genes. Siblings are more closely related to each other than they are to their parents (unless they are half siblings). (Interesting aside regarding half siblings– they are more common in the population than you know! Researchers have to consider this fact when they do their studies.) There are also grandparents, aunts, uncles and cousins all sharing certain amounts of genes. The more genes in common, the more genetic disorders in common.

Studies of adopted children yield useful information about genetics. Studies of children raised by non-biologic relatives allow issues of genes verses environment to be sorted out. Studies of identical twins adopted by non-relatives and raised apart are the best. Adopted identical twins raised by non-relatives can be compared with adopted non-identical (fraternal) twins. Since fraternal twins can be either same sex or opposite sex, studies comparing fraternal and identical twins can detect differential effects of genes and environment on boys and girls. What happens to a child without a genetic background for antisocial personality disorder or addiction who is adopted into a family where one or both of the parents has these disorders? What happens to the biologic child of one or two affected parents raised by non-relatives in a good environment? Do genes and environment affect boys and girls in the same way? Science has provided us with answers to these questions and more.

There have now been several large-scale family studies, adoption studies and twin studies.[1] These studies reveal that there is a strong genetic component to antisocial behavior. Several surprising and somewhat confusing findings have also emerged. A comparison of the estimates of the genetic component of adult antisocial behavior with that of childhood antisocial behavior shows that genes actually exert a stronger influence over the final outcome in adulthood, than over this behavior during childhood.[2] These studies also suggest there are two sets of genes that determine antisocial personality traits. One set is present during early childhood and the other set is activated at puberty. These genes appear to be the same for males and females.

It has been suggested that a woman with antisocial personality disorder carries stronger genes for the disorder than does a man. This idea is supported by the observation that genetic transmission of antisocial personality disorder is most likely if the affected parent is the **biologic** mother.[3] The genetic component of childhood antisocial behavior is also much larger for girls than it is for boys.[4] However, studies show that boys "catch up" and that in adulthood the genetic component of antisocial behavior increases for males. Prevalence studies indicate that antisocial personality disorder is more common in men than women.[5] Therefore, some researchers have concluded that boys are more sensitive to negative early environments.[6]

The above research suggests that as we think about genetic risk we have to consider that genes related to antisocial behavior may be activated at different time points from birth to adolescence to adulthood. The environmental factors that influence behavior may also change over the course of development. Infants and young children may be more sensitive to environmental toxins. Since teens play a larger role in selecting their own friends than do young children, genetics may determine social environment for teens more than for children. Teens with genetically influenced behavior problems tend to seek each other out. They then influence each other, magnifying the apparent genetic component.[7]

Does addiction in general tend to run in families, or is it the preference for a given substance of abuse that is inherited? Studies indicate that some forms of alcoholism are inherited as a specific problem with alcohol and not addiction in general.[8] Abuse of other substances and antisocial personality do not seem to run together in all families of alcoholics. A cluster of disorders does exist in many families of alcoholics. That cluster includes abuse of many substances, addiction in general, childhood antisocial behavior, ADHD, teenage onset of substance abuse, and adult antisocial personality disorder.[9]

In one adoption study, adopted children were selected for examination if a biologic parent had antisocial personality disorder or substance abuse.[10] Most of the biologic parents with substance abuse were alcoholics. When both biologic parents were free of these disorders, children generally did well. Children whose **biologic parents** had substance abuse disorders or antisocial personality were most at risk to develop these disorders. Furthermore, impulsive-aggressive personality traits were genetically transmitted and placed children at risk (more on impulsivity and aggression later).[11]

There is little doubt that ADHD symptoms are genetically transmitted in families.[12] It appears that the same genes that increase risk for ADHD also increase risk for antisocial personality[13] and addiction. Antisocial behavior is common in children with ADHD.[14] Teens with ADHD are at high risk for addiction.[15] The biologic relatives of children with ADHD often have antisocial personality traits and addiction.[16] Since there are some ADHD families with no increase in addiction and antisocial personality, the exact nature of the common bond between these disorders is unknown.

The Prevention of a Disorder– The Reason to Worry About Who Is At Risk

There is a very good reason to worry about who is at risk for disorders. **Knowing who is at risk makes prevention possible.** The field of public health defines three different kinds of prevention. The first, called primary prevention, is illustrated by the following example. In the first two years of life, your child's pediatrician will perform a lead screening by checking for lead in your child's blood. Does the pediatrician order a lead screening because he believes your child has lead poisoning? No, all children have lead levels checked in order to prevent lead poisoning from ever happening in the first place. A child with high lead levels can be symptom free for a long time. If we can find children who have high lead levels but are symptom free, we can prevent illness due to lead poisoning.

Primary prevention is the form of prevention most of us call prevention, i.e. keeping an illness or disorder from ever happening. Doctors or public health officials perform a screening test, identify children at risk due to the results of that test, then take specific steps to prevent the disorder in those children. This primary prevention is the subject I am most concerned with. Unfortunately, there is as yet no simple screening test available for identifying children at risk for antisocial personality disorder, addiction and/or ADHD.

What do scientific studies tell us about which children are most at risk for antisocial personality disorder, addiction and/or ADHD? The Diagnostic and Statistical Manual of Mental Disorders put out by the American Psychiatric Association (DSM IV) makes the following statement: "Adopted-away children resemble their biological parents more than their adoptive parents, but the adoptive family environment influences the risk of developing a personality disorder." As I discussed in the prior section, there are many studies of twins and adopted children showing that genetics increases risk for antisocial personality, addiction and ADHD. Furthermore, the biologic relatives of those with antisocial personality disorder are also at increased risk to develop substance abuse disorders and ADHD.

I suggest that **at risk** children be identified as those who are genetically related to others known to have these disorders. Specific prevention efforts can then be targeted toward these at risk children. **Since the background of adopted children may be unknown, I believe that these children should be raised as if they are at risk.** Special care could save a great deal of later grief. The list of at risk children therefore includes the biologic sons, daughters, nieces, nephews and grandchildren of persons with antisocial personality, addition and/or ADHD. Prevention of antisocial personality disorder, addiction and ADHD in **at risk** children should begin in the first five years of life. Prevention efforts in the first five years ensure the best chance of preventing any manifestation of these disorders.

Life is difficult and certainly not perfect, and many parents will not begin prevention efforts until after age five, therefore, I also address secondary prevention in this book. Secondary prevention entails preventing the full development of a disorder once some aspects of that disorder are already there. Using the lead-screening example, say due to an oversight, your child missed his lead screening, and you later had questions about his speech development. When you shared these concerns with your pediatrician, he said, "Your child never had his lead screening, we had better check a lead level right away." When your child's lead level came back high, treatment for lead poisoning began immediately. This treatment hopefully reversed the bad effects of the poison on your child's development. I believe secondary prevention of antisocial personality, addiction and ADHD is possible. Some children do show early signs of developing greater risk for these problems. You will learn what these signs are and what to do in response to these signs.

The third type of prevention is tertiary prevention. Tertiary prevention involves preventing complications once a full disorder has revealed itself. For antisocial personality disorder, this is no later than age 15. Young people with antisocial personality disorder are usually not upset at having the disorder. Thus, they seek treatment only when coerced, usually by parents or the legal system. Since behavior change requires a person willing to change, tertiary prevention in the usual sense is not possible. For this disorder, tertiary prevention involves protecting other people from the complications of the disorder. Unfortunately, incarceration is the most frequent form of tertiary prevention of antisocial behavior.

If it were true that a child's fate is determined at birth or shortly thereafter, there would be no reason for this book. It is clear that antisocial personality and related disorders develop as the result of an interaction between genetics and early environment. This interaction occurs in three specific areas that I have called the **Inner Triangle**. The development of antisocial personality and related disorders happens when children are born with vulnerabilities in one, two or three sides of the triangle. **A child born with severe vulnerability in all three sides of the Inner Triangle will require extraordinary parenting just to be "OK."**

CHAPTER 2

THE INNER TRIANGLE

Antisocial Personality Disorder and the Inner Triangle

Three percent of the population,[17] or about 8,100,000 individuals in the United States have antisocial personality disorder. Even more people have antisocial personality traits but not the full disorder. What is antisocial personality and how does it develop? Antisocial personality disorder is the official term for a syndrome that has also been called sociopathy. The term psychopath is used to refer to individuals with an extreme form of this same disorder. A committee of experts has developed the current, most accepted definition of antisocial personality disorder. Antisocial personality disorder is described in DSM IV as "a pervasive pattern of disregard for and violation of the rights of others occurring since age 15 as indicated by three or more of the following:

1) Failure to conform to social norms with respect to lawful behaviors as indicated by repeatedly performing acts that are grounds for arrest.

2) Deceitfulness, as indicated by repeatedly lying, use of aliases or conning others for personal profit or pleasure.

3) Impulsivity or failure to plan ahead.

4) Irritability and aggressiveness, as indicated by repeated physical fights or assaults.

5) Reckless disregard for safety of self or others.

6) Consistent irresponsibility, as indicated by repeated failure to sustain consistent work behavior or honor financial obligations.

7) Lack of remorse, as indicated by being indifferent to or rationalizing having hurt, mistreated, or stolen from another.

Consider how early in life this disorder is already fully formed! A person does not have to be a criminal to meet criteria for antisocial personality disorder. There is a broad spectrum of severity of this disorder. An irritable, aggressive, reckless individual who is irresponsible and habitually lies is classified as having antisocial personality disorder. An impulsive person with irresponsible work behavior and no remorse for his bad actions also has antisocial personality.

Regardless of severity, as a group, these individuals are NOT otherwise "normal" people who make bad moral choices. Individuals with this disorder have an abnormal emotional life. They are "glib" "superficial" and "shallow." They have little or no capacity for empathy,[18] and no conscience (criterion 7). The lack of empathy and absence of conscience allows them to disregard the rights of others. Researchers have developed scales and have actually measured what they call "emotional callousness" in individuals with antisocial personality disorder.[19] Perhaps due to the lack of emotional connection and absence of the ability to put themselves in other people's shoes, those with antisocial personality are also grandiose and self-centered.

Because they do not feel emotions, individuals with antisocial personality disorder respond to reward and punishment differently from the rest of us. Research shows their autonomic nervous system is actually under active at rest.[20] Because of this low arousal, these individuals have an increased need for excitement and are driven by uncontrollable impulses. The increased need for excitement and poor response to punishment sets the stage for substance abuse and addiction (more on this later).

Imagine a triangle with three sides representing the three qualities that serve to form character.[21] These qualities, that form the basis of character are, **ability to love**, **ability to control impulses**, and **moral reasoning ability**. Those with antisocial personality have a severe disorder of character. **At the core of antisocial personality is a deficit in all three sides of the Inner Triangle.**

Because individuals with antisocial personality disorder are unable to love, it is easy for them to pursue a lifestyle of exploitation of others (criterion 5 and 7). They have little or no ability to control their impulses (criterion 1, 3 and 4). They also lack a moral code to live by (criterion 1, 2, 6). In this book, you will learn how these problems develop and you will learn a strategy for preventing these problems in your **at risk** child.

Think about what character means. Character is the **ability to love**, the ability to control impulses and moral reasoning ability. A person with good character is strong in all three qualities. The base of the Inner Triangle and the core of good character is the **ability to love**. **Ability to love** is dependent on our inner emotional life and capacity for empathy (Chapter 3). The sides of the triangle are formed by ability to control impulses (Chapter 4) and moral reasoning ability (Chapter 5). Impulse control involves suppressing and managing urges and feelings. Moral reasoning ability is our cognitive understanding of morality and the way we use this understanding. A person with **ability to love** and good impulse control would function well in any society, regardless of that society's moral values. Moral values vary, depending on culture, however all human societies have a moral code members are expected to live by.

To better understand how the Inner Triangle works, let us look at what the result would be if only one of the three sides was poorly developed. A person with little **ability to love** would be the most impaired. However, a person with little empathy and impoverished emotional life could partially compensate with strong impulse control and strong moral reasoning ability. His moral values and self-control would tell him to behave in a good way toward others, even if he lacked feelings to guide his behavior. I am sure you know someone who fits this description. Often these people are somewhat cold individuals who must "play everything by the book." Because they lack strong loving feelings to guide their behavior, they realistically fear what would happen if their impulse control and/or moral reasoning ability deteriorated.

These "play it by the book" individuals are experienced by others as constricted in the area of feelings. Nevertheless, they are generally good people who do not exploit others. Thus, some interaction between genes and upbringing can allow for the development of a character where weakness in **ability to love** is balanced by good impulse control and good moral reasoning ability. *I say keep playing by the book. That is a very good thing.*

A person with poor impulse control but with well-developed **ability to love** and moral reasoning ability is a guilty, remorseful, but impulsive person. These individuals do bad things on impulse even though they do not really want to. Because this type of person is disturbed by the problem, he is likely to seek help. Those with poor impulse control benefit from training and medication to strengthen their impulse control center.

When **ability to love** and impulse control are relatively intact and moral reasoning ability is impaired, bad actions seem justified to the individual that does them. This is why we use the saying "there is honor among thieves." Thieves with honor have intact **ability to love**. Many people who end up in the criminal justice system get there because of impaired moral reasoning and impaired impulse control.

In my opinion, we should develop reliable ways to identify criminals who have intact **ability to love**. These individuals would not meet criterion 7 of DSM IV. The problem is that remorse is very hard to measure, and many with antisocial personality disorder pretend to be remorseful. Moral reasoning ability can be improved through education and treatment in a person who is otherwise intact. The increase in criminal behavior found in lower socioeconomic groups is not only due to an increase in true antisocial personality disorder in these groups. Instead, differences in moral reasoning ability and parental training of impulse control are to blame.

Those with antisocial personality disorder have poor **ability to love**, poor impulse control, and a low moral reasoning ability. These individuals do not just wake up at age 15 and come down with the disorder as if they caught a cold. The problems with **ability to love**, **impulse control** and **moral reasoning ability** develop from the time of conception. I will contend that there is likely a *critical period* for the development of the **ability to love. Impulse control** and **moral reasoning ability** can be improved upon at any age, provided a person is motivated to try. **Development of the ability to love sets the stage for development of impulse control and moral reasoning ability.**

A critical period is a developmental age during which experience must act on the brain in order to create the proper wiring. During a critical period, the brain is uniquely sensitive to environmental input, and experience can direct the formation of connections between cells. Although experience can modify connections outside a critical period, the degree of change possible is much less than during a critical period. The important point is that early experiences profoundly affect the structure of the child's brain, and these experiences have less of an effect on the adult brain. Much greater experiential input is required to facilitate change in an adult as compared to a child.

Our best understanding of critical periods in brain development comes from studies of the visual system.[22] These studies show that experience strengthens some pathways of brain cell connections. Cells whose pathways are not strengthened by experience fail to make proper connections and may even die. **In other words, lack of proper stimulation causes permanent damage to the wiring of the brain.** In humans, certain visual pathways in the brain must be strengthened by the right kind of visual stimulation by age 9 or normal vision does not develop.

Is there evidence for a critical period for the development of **ability to love**? The answer is an unequivocal yes. The literature is so extensive that the brief summary I can give here cannot really do the topic justice. In a beautifully written paper *The Nature of a Child's Tie to His Mother*, John Bowlby[23] first made us think about the devastating consequences maternal deprivation has on humans. Maternal deprivation and separation can damage an individual for life. Mary Ainsworth[24] and other researchers have used experiments to measure the effect that a child's early relationship with his mother has on personality. Research has clearly shown a direct link between a child's early relationship with his mother and later emotional functioning. Without an early secure attachment to mother or primary caregiver, the **ability to love** is permanently impaired.

An interplay between inborn qualities and early experience is responsible for a child's **ability to love**. Some children, call them resilient children, are born with a great capacity to receive love input from mother and develop the brain connections necessary to become loving adults. Other children, call them vulnerable children, are born with reduced capacity to turn love input into the proper brain wiring. If we consider that antisocial personality is inherited as a vulnerability to maternal deprivation and rejection, we can begin to see the complex ways genes and environment work together. If the vulnerability is very strong, the substrate in the child the nurturing mother has to work with is greatly reduced. A child may experience deprivation even if his mother tries to be present for him. **Thus, large amounts of the right kind of nurturance will be required for the proper development of ability to love in an at risk child.** Lack of **ability to love** can occur in children even when families provide nurturance. **Perhaps for a few unlucky children, no amount of nurturance can fully compensate for extreme inborn vulnerability.**

Some parents are blessed with easy kids. There are some resilient individuals born with very low vulnerability to antisocial personality. These children can be raised in the harshest environments and still develop the capacity for love and empathy. When we examine antisocial personality disorder in relation to socioeconomic status we have to acknowledge that since, statistically, children of poverty are more likely to experience neglect and deprivation; those that overcome these early experiences must have very low vulnerability. That the rates of antisocial personality in disadvantaged groups are not even higher, speaks to the resilience of the best in the human spirit.

"You can't teach an old dog new tricks," is a common saying that testifies to the fact that there may be a critical period for training **impulse control**. Most who have been parents or have spent time around young children, know that **impulse control** generally improves with age but varies among children of the same age. **Impulse control** may temporarily decline during early puberty. Girls generally have more **impulse control** and develop it faster than do boys. Research shows that the brain structures involved in **impulse control** continue to develop at least into the early 20's.[25] A motivated adult can improve his **impulse control** with training and practice. However, everything else being equal, children whose parents train them to control their impulses do better and have an easier time as adults.

Teaching **impulse control** is an important part of parenting. Just as some children are born with vulnerability in the area of the **ability to love**, others suffer with extremely poor **impulse control**. Training these children to control their impulses is very difficult. Inborn trouble with **impulse control** is a large part of the cause of the link between antisocial personality disorder, addiction and ADHD. There is another, less known childhood behavioral disorder, oppositional defiant disorder (ODD). This disorder is also caused by poor **impulse control** (Chapter 4).

The development of **moral reasoning ability** is a complex subject and has been well described in other books.[26] The point I wish to emphasize is that **moral reasoning ability** changes with age in line with intellectual development. The ability to reason morally is therefore dependent on brain structure and intelligence. If a child lacks general intelligence, then higher levels of **moral reasoning ability** may not be possible. Furthermore, development of **ability to love** and **impulse control** directly affect moral development. Of all three sides of the Inner Triangle, **moral reasoning ability** is the most flexible. Growth in **moral reasoning ability** can continue throughout life, provided a person is motivated to work on himself.

Addiction and the Inner Triangle

The American Psychiatric Association's DSM IV does not recognize the term addiction. Instead, the term substance dependence is used. Many psychiatrists (myself included) use the term addiction because addiction is different from dependence. A cancer patient who takes strong painkillers to relieve pain will likely become physically dependent on these substances. This physical dependence that occurs in everyone exposed for long duration to these drugs is not the same as addiction. Addiction involves much more than physical or even psychological dependence.

Addiction entails the pursuit of intoxication with a substance irrespective of the negative consequences to self and family. Putting a discussion of cause and effect relationships aside for the moment, addiction is also associated with impairment in all three sides of the Inner Triangle. **Ability to love, impulse control** and **moral reasoning ability** are all reduced in addiction (and perhaps also by addiction).

Adolescents and adults addicted to substances have impaired **ability to love**. With addiction comes blunted feelings and lack of empathy. Callous exploitation of others becomes a way of life for addicts. They behave as if nothing and no one matters as much as intoxication. Mothers even abandon their children to use drugs.

Impairment of **impulse control** occurs with addiction. One of the criteria for substance dependence is the inability to fight an impulse to use a substance even when the substance dependent person wants to stop. Young people who have not developed **impulse control** are at great risk to become addicts if they happen to try an addicting substance. Treatment of addiction involves improving **impulse control**.

Moral reasoning ability declines with addiction, as addicts stop believing in moral values they once held dear. Many, addicted individuals engage in criminal behavior in order to obtain their substance of choice. This behavior puts them in a position of having to justify their actions. Addicts use a multitude of rationalizations to support their lifestyle of gaining substances at the expense of everything and everyone else.

I trained in psychiatry at a large teaching hospital in Los Angeles County where I evaluated and treated many patients with addiction. Like many of my colleagues, I was astounded by what appeared to be the high prevalence of antisocial personality traits in addicted persons. Could it be that the antisocial personality traits preceded addiction in ALL these people? The family members of addicts and alcoholics answered my question. Many maintained that addiction had changed the patient. Before starting the substance, the addict was a loving, contributing family member. Addiction made him callous, impulsive and immoral. It is as if the over-use of alcohol and some drugs damages the brain centers involved in maintaining the Inner Triangle.

ADHD and the Inner Triangle

DSM IV states, "The essential feature of attention deficit hyperactivity disorder is a persistent pattern of inattention and/or hyperactivity-impulsivity that is more frequently displayed and more severe than is typically observed in individuals at a comparable level of development." The prevalence of ADHD is 3-7% of school-aged children. Like antisocial personality disorder and some forms of alcoholism, ADHD is more frequent in males than in females. Unlike antisocial personality disorder and addiction, ADHD is associated with impairment in only one side of the Inner Triangle.

Children and adults with ADHD have intact **ability to love** and may have age appropriate **moral reasoning ability**. Impairment in **impulse control** defines and causes this disorder. As will be discussed more fully later, the ability to sustain attention is directly related to **impulse control**. The brain produces many different ideas of what to do, think and feel. Correct behavior requires filtering of these ideas and work to stay on task. This filtering and the ability to stay on task are impaired in ADHD.

Nature Verses Nurture

To summarize the current thought on nature verses nurture as pertains to the brain and behavior. An individual is born with a potential defined by his genes. That potential can yield a range of outcomes depending on **childhood** experience. For the genetically **at risk** child, behavioral outcomes in adulthood can range from unaffected, to slightly affected, to devastating antisocial personality disorder and addiction.

Because the genes determining adult antisocial behavior may not be activated until adolescence, the effects of early childhood experience may not be seen until adolescence. Since I know my child may have been born with a diminished capacity to enjoy love and feel loved, it follows that he may be extraordinarily sensitive to depravation and rejection especially in early childhood. The **at risk** child may also have more problems developing impulse control. Moral reasoning ability may not be the **at risk** child's strongest suit. It is my solemn duty as his mother to do everything I can to optimally raise him and see that he fulfills *his* developmental potential. **My at risk child's developmental needs may be different from those of other children.**

A woman I deeply respect is a woman of faith, an attorney, and child advocate. I have known her since before her youngest son was born. He is now 14. She is an attentive mother who realized early on that her son was "different." He seemed delayed in some aspects of his physical and social development. She had the wisdom and dedication to quit her job in order to attend to the needs of her son. (Fortunately, she also has a husband who is able to provide for his family.) As I watched that boy grow up, there was no doubt in my mind that his mother's close attention made it possible for him to realize his full potential. With the good start she gave him, that boy will be able to live a good life.

If you are with me in being entrusted with the care of an **at risk** child, please stop to recognize that raising him may require a good deal more effort than you expected. The demands that raising an **at risk** child places on a parent are considerable. Take inventory of what you are willing to give up for the sake of your child. How/what can you compromise in order to have more time for your child? Are there other relationships (perhaps romantic) or activities that are draining you and taking you away from your precious child? What supports have you built into your life to keep you strong? How do you renew yourself and increase your capacity for patience? Remember, raising this child is going to require a total commitment until he is at least 15 years old.

Please resolve to retake inventory of your life every few months as circumstances change. Have the strength to eliminate influences that impair your ability to parent. If you suffer with depression or anxiety, get help. Stop smoking, exercise and eat right. Raising your child is going to take the very best you have to offer!

CHAPTER 3

YOUR CHILD'S ABILITY TO LOVE

What Is Ability to Love?

Love is the glue that binds us together as social creatures. Since we humans are so social, the **ability to love** is very important to us as a species. Without love, instead of being together, we would all be loners and seek to live solitary lives. Without love, mothers and fathers would not care for children, husbands and wives would not stay together, and none of us would have any friends. In fact, for most of us, the **ability to love** is so much a part of who we are, that we take love for granted, and don't even stop to consider what it is.

Just what is the nature of this love glue that binds us together? Scientists have attempted to answer this question several ways. They have studied social animals, and have tried to understand what holds animal groups together. They have also studied disordered humans— people who seem to lack the glue. Studies of animals show that love-glue has at least four different ingredients. The first ingredient is called "proximity seeking." Those that love, tend to stick physically close to each other. The second ingredient involves identifying and preferring special individuals to seek proximity to. The third ingredient involves pleasure. Social creatures greatly enjoy being close to each other. The fourth ingredient involves pain. Pain is caused by separation from and loss of, loved ones.

Stop and think for a moment, about the ingredients of love. If you have ever had a dog you will agree with what I am about to say. My dog follows me everywhere I go! There is no doubt she knows who I am. If there are other people with us, she looks around to find me, and comes right to me. She greatly enjoys my presence. When she finds me, she barks happily and wags her tail. She is sad when I leave her, and desperately attempts to follow. If I did not crate her, she would claw and dig her way out of the house. If my dog sensed my life was in danger, she would try to save me, even if that meant risking her own life. My dog loves me.

Scientists have defined the relationship characterized by a tendency to seek proximity to a specific, special other. This relationship is called an attachment. A person shows he has an attachment to another person if he strongly desires to be with that person.

One of the interesting things about attachment is that it is to some degree neutral with regard to pleasure and pain. There are conditions under which animals will form attachments even if those attachments do not cause them much pleasure. Attachments also sometimes form even if they cause pain. This pleasure/pain neutral characteristic of attachment is also seen in humans. Women often stick by abusive husbands, and remarkably, some children seem to love abusive parents.

What good does it serve for attachment to be pleasure/pain neutral? It is very important that attachment is pleasure/pain neutral. Even in loving relationships, there is some degree of competition. This competition or struggle for dominance sometimes causes pain. If attachments depended on positive feelings or pleasure, then we would all part company after the first fight. We would not stay together very long!

There are people who are so disordered that they do not form attachments (except to perhaps one or two family members). These people are called schizoid personalities. The development of schizoid personality disorder is strongly influenced by genetics. This disorder shows us that the human ability to form attachments is inborn and dependent on inheritance. Most babies are born with a strong tendency to attach to mother. This tendency allows them to survive in a dangerous world.

Love is much more than attachment, however. Antisocial personality disorder and some other personality disorders teach us what happens when attachment is the only ingredient of relationships. Those with antisocial personality disorder and addiction form attachments but have impaired **ability to love.** This impairment prevents them from forming caring, loving relationships. Those with antisocial personality generally lack feelings of affection. Their lifestyle is characterized by exploitation, rather than caretaking of those with whom they have attachments. It is affectionate, empathetic, caretaking behavior that is impaired in both addiction and antisocial personality disorder.

In addition to attachment, love involves feelings of affection, empathy, and caretaking behavior. In part, it is our enjoyment of attachments that leads us to be empathetic, kind and altruistic. Thus, our **ability to love** is limited by the degree to which we are able to enjoy other people. Remember I said that a person with relatively low **ability to love** can partially compensate with strong **impulse control** and **strong moral reasoning ability**? What I meant was that a person who does not really enjoy relationships can still behave in a loving way if he believes it is his duty to do so, and he has enough will power. Will power enables kind, altruistic behavior to stem from a sense of duty, rather than from feelings of affection. Since, our ability to enjoy feelings of affection fluctuates so much over the course of our lives; we must be able to behave in a loving way even when we do not particularly feel like it. The importance of a sense of duty and will power (or **impulse control**) cannot be understated (more on these later).

Parents often take for granted that children will naturally develop into loving young people without much intervention. This is in part because in the absence of severe trauma children generally enjoy life and other people. This innocent enjoyment makes children more loving than adults. Sadly, for many children, enjoyment is stamped out during childhood. Other children lack this temperamental joyfulness. Again, when enjoyment wanes, we are left to fall back on morality and will power to tell us to behave kindly.

Ability to Love

A person with ability to love does all of the following:

1) He seeks to be physically close to and spend time with special others.

2) He enjoys having affectionate feelings toward these special people.

3) He shows empathy toward those he loves.

4) He experiences a compulsion to take care of those he loves.

5) He at times sacrifices his own desires in order to provide for a loved person.

The ability to love is tied to, and cannot be separated from, the capacity for: closeness and proximity seeking, feeling in

general, joy and empathy. Your child first shows he is developing the **ability to love** when he cries to be close to you even when his physical needs are met. Then, after he can crawl or walk on his own, he still seeks to be close to you, especially when he is tired or afraid. These behaviors demonstrate that the **ability to love** starts with a habit of seeking proximity to mom and dad. This habit of proximity seeking begins in the first year of life.

Young children that have secure attachments to their parents seek to be near them, especially when distressed. Parents then become a base from which secure children launch missions of exploration of their world. In **at risk** children, the drive to explore is so strong that proximity seeking behavior is reduced. **It is as if the at risk child does not require a parental base in the same way other children do.** The parents of the **at risk** child have to take an active role in encouraging the child to remain close. Too much independence or premature independence is not good for the **at risk** child. He needs to learn to slow down and enjoy the rewards of closeness with loved ones. Furthermore, there is a real risk of physical injury should the toddler wander too far from his mother.

Since being loving involves experiencing feelings of affection and warmth toward others; **we want our children to develop a habit of identifying and greatly enjoying feelings of warmth and affection.** To maintain a proper life balance the enjoyment of loving feelings must be as important as the enjoyment of other activities. One of the core problems in antisocial personality disorder is a lack of balance in pleasure (p. 144). Those with antisocial personality derive more pleasure from "thrill seeking" and other forms of entertainment than they do from their attachments; this is why they can throw attachments away if the impulse arises.

In addition to having attachments to immediate family members, it is important for children to learn thoughtful caretaking of loved persons. Not that I advocate a reversal of the one way parent-child relationship, but a child should show concern for the well-being of his parents and those in his family. In the school-aged child, caretaking of family and friends may involve putting his own needs and desires aside for a time. For this and other reasons, the **ability to love** is partially limited by the degree of **impulse control** a person possesses.

The first step toward maximizing the **ability to love** in your child is to realize that **ability to love** makes the person. Ask yourself if deep down you believe that the ability to be a feeling, caring and empathetic person is as important for males as it is for females. It may seem unnatural to train a boy to be loving. Think about finding male role models for your son who demonstrate that a man can be sensitive without losing his manliness. There are likely many true gentlemen in your family and community. Examples are also found in books, and throughout history; many great men have exemplified the character of a loving man.

The Dash

I read of a man who stood to speak
at the funeral of his friend
He referred to the dates on her tombstone
from the beginning...to the end.

He noted that first came the date of her birth
and spoke of the second with tears,
but he said that what mattered most of all
Was the dash between the years.

For that dash represents all the time
that she spent alive on Earth
and now only those who loved her
know what that little line is worth.
For it matters not, how much we own
the cars..the house...the cash

*What matters most is how we live and love
and how we spend our dash.*

*So think about this long and hard
are there things you'd like to change?
For you never know how much time is left
that can still be rearranged.'*

*If we could just slow down enough
to consider what's true and what's real
and always try to understand
the way other people feel.*

*And be less quick to anger
and show appreciation more
and love the people in our lives
like we've never loved before.*

*If we treat each other with respect
and more often wear a smile
remembering that special dash
might only last a little while.*

*So when your eulogy is being read
with your life's actions to rehash
Would you be pleased with the things
they have to say,
About how you spent your dash?**

---

*"The Dash" by Linda Ellis, Copyright 1996 Linda Ellis, www.lindaellis.net.

The second step to increasing your child's **ability to love** is to realize that this ability will not come automatically without effort. Children, especially **at risk** children, need the right kind of parenting or they will not fully develop the **ability to love**. Your child's **ability to love** will be strongly influenced by how you raise him.

The **ability to love** is like any other talent where inborn ability is important, but has to be followed by practice. For example, your child may have been born with musical talent, but if you do not provide him with an instrument to practice on, he will never learn to play. Even a child with little or no inborn musical talent can learn to play an instrument with the right teaching and enough practice. Learning to love also involves teaching and practice. Thus, **at risk** children can only develop the **ability to love** if you provide them with the right teaching and an instrument to practice. The teaching comes from you. You are also the instrument your child relies on for practice.

Given that you have decided with me to make developing the **ability to love** the top priority, then trying to encourage other qualities will have to take a back seat. These other qualities may be desirable but not as desirable since choices have to be made. For example, **ability to love** is of greater value than being competitive and more important than developing the desire to be dominant. Being loving is more important than being analytical. A dominant, competitive and analytical man is generally more highly regarded than is a gentle, empathetic man. I am asking you to do the opposite of what you, society and your family may want.

Keep in mind that when a child is naturally talented in a given area, he will tend to gravitate toward activities that maximize his strengths. An athletic child will want to play sports. An intelligent child will become absorbed in reading and mathematics. A child resists spending time developing parts of himself that are more difficult. Since your **at risk** child may have been born with an increased desire for dominance and a tendency to be aggressive, he may naturally want to focus on these. For example, your at "risk child" may be preoccupied with competitiveness in everything he does. He may also be physically aggressive and preoccupied with martial arts. An excessive focus on dominance and aggression impairs **ability to love.**

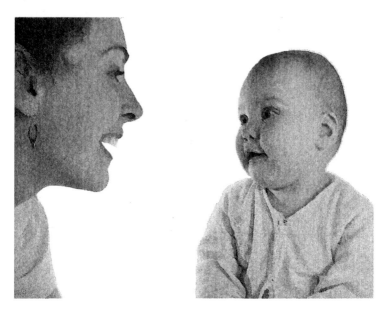

"My child you must learn to enjoy feelings, even if entering the feeling realm does not come easily for you. "

Birth to 12 Months

The development of the **ability to love** begins before a child is born. Please, if your child has not yet been born, obtain prenatal care, eat right and refrain from cigarettes, drugs and alcohol. Studies have shown that smoking during pregnancy and birth trauma increase subsequent risk for antisocial personality disorder.[27] Follow your doctor's advice to minimize trauma to your baby during delivery. Do not resist C-section if your doctor recommends it.

Learning to love begins in infancy as the infant develops a habit of enjoying being held. Many child care experts believe that breast-feeding strengthens the bond between mother and infant. Breast-fed infants receive 8-12 feedings each day for the first six weeks. This amounts to 338+ opportunities for holding and cuddling in comparison to 216 for the bottle-fed infant fed every four hours. Thus, in the first six weeks, breast-fed infants potentially receive more physical contact than do bottle-fed infants. Since breast-feeding also provides the best nutrients for baby, breast-feeding is highly recommended for **at risk** infants. Caregivers of bottle-fed infants should make an extra effort to hold them.

Consider putting your baby in a front carrier and holding him close much of the day. This carrying behavior has been part of human history since our time on Earth began. Develop a habit of holding. A few hours of holding each day can make a big difference for your baby. A child held for two hours each day from age 2-8 months receives 360 hours of close human contact. During these hours, important brain connections form. On the other hand, a baby who is not held forms all his brain connections while lying in his crib.

Holding and playing with an eight month old is different from holding a two-month-old infant. The idea is to provide physical contact and comfort to the small baby. The older infant needs fun play along with physical comfort.

It is now understood that families from different cultures have different attitudes toward the holding of infants. Embedded in these attitudes is the wisdom that **even babies form habits that guide their behavior.**[28] Unfortunately, some practices that arise from these attitudes start babies down a path of aloofness rather than down a path of joy in loving. I have heard well-meaning relatives of young mothers warn, "Don't hold that baby too much or he'll cry every time you put him down!" Our goal for the **at risk** baby is for him to become so accustomed to holding that he at times does cry when his mother puts him down. We want him to prefer the embrace of his mother to the feel of his infant seat or crib. He must begin early the habit of human tenderness.

Between four weeks and three months of age, some infants develop "colic" and/or "irritable crying." There is some disagreement over whether these conditions are the same or different. Treatments for these conditions are evolving so check with your health care provider. "Irritable crying" which occurs at about the same time every day and may last hours, is due to immaturity of the nervous system. I mention this condition for two reasons. First, this condition is very nerve-racking for parents and can set the stage for a negative parent-child relationship. Second, babies with irritable crying may do better if they are not held during the time of day they have their crying spells. Swaddling with light blankets and placement in a quiet place may be the best solution for irritable crying spells.

One summer, a new single mother stayed with our family for a time. Her three-month-old baby, a girl, had irritable crying. The poor mother was up late the first night she stayed with us, trying to sooth her crying infant. She tried feeding, changing, pacifier, rocking and singing and the baby would still not stop crying. I did not want to interfere with my guests care of her own child but I worried she was becoming emotionally and physically exhausted. I got up and asked, "Did the hospital show you how to swaddle your baby?" I then took the little girl, wrapped her in a receiving blanket, and put her in her crib. She immediately calmed and went to sleep. From then on, her mother used this strategy in the evening to head off the crying spells. A great deal of frustration and anguish was prevented. If you suspect that your child has colic or irritable crying, seek consultation and support regarding how best to help him.

Our goal for the first year of life is for baby to develop a strong sense of his mother (and father). We want baby to prefer his mother (and father) to other people and to find special comfort in her embrace. Therefore, to the extent possible keep the number of different caregivers low. If you have to be away from baby, keep a T-shirt you have worn in his crib. Babies seem to derive comfort from the smell of their mothers. If you are working, encourage the day-care staff to allow long naps, so your child will be alert for you in the evening. Spend time holding your child and playing with him. He is more important than a clean house or other priorities.

By 4-6 months of age, infants have developed head control and can sit up to manipulate objects with their hands. At this age, it is important to begin reading to your child and encouraging him to play with objects. Reading to your child develops important language skills and teaches him that humans enjoy learning together. Manipulating objects encourages the development of handedness. Both handedness and verbal ability are related to a brain development called cerebral dominance. Cerebral dominance means that one side of the brain takes over the job of doing certain tasks. Some have speculated that this specialization is defective in persons with antisocial personality disorder. Early stimulation could be important in over coming this developmental problem.

Plan to spend a few minutes each day playing games with your child that will help him with his motor development. Some little ones relate physically more readily than they do verbally. Thus, physical games will seal the connection with a non-verbal child. Hold his hands while he practices walking. Tickle him; play with his hands and feet as he lies on his back. Connect the verbal with the physical as early as possible by teaching him the meaning of "give me a hug" and "give me a kiss."

I noticed early on that my son preferred singing to the spoken word. Starting at about 10 months, I taught him a simple tune "I love ma-ma." I sang it at times **he initiated** affection toward me. He could hum the tune before he could say the words. He learned to use this tune to connect with his own loving feelings. He later changed "ma-ma" to the names of other family members and our pets. Children develop an appreciation of music very early.[29] I believe this appreciation can be used to tie together the emotional, verbal and physical realms (through dancing). The point is to use every possible tool to connect with your child and give him joy.

Connecting in the first year (as well as later on) depends on **responsiveness.**[30] Being **responsive** means being sensitive to your child's moods, needs, and desires both expressed and unexpressed. This sensitivity should guide your behavior toward your child. Although I advocate that caregivers play a very active role with **at risk** children, I do not encourage overwhelming them (see p. 62). Children also need a chance to initiate interactions and explore the environment on their own. If you sense your child needs quiet time on his own, don't be afraid to let him alone to play for a while. Similarly, if you are busy with an activity, and he cries for you, make it a point to **respond** to his cries, even if just for a moment. **Avoid at all costs a habit of ignoring your child. Your child needs the empowering knowledge that he can ask for you and you will be there.**

How to Be More Responsive to Your Child

Empathy is the force that drives mothers and fathers to be **responsive** to their children. When parents are stressed, empathy becomes a luxury, not a way of life. To have more empathy, get rid of the stresses you can eliminate, and learn to cope with the stress you cannot get rid of. Studies show that stress reduction improves parenting.[31] Take care of YOUR physical health. Get enough sleep, eat right and exercise regularly.

Sources of stress include relationships with other adults, financial worries and misplaced priorities. Stop a moment and take inventory of your adult relationships. Are there friends, lovers or family members who are draining you? Ask yourself if any draining relationships are really more important to you than the well-being of your child. Resolve either to spend less time with draining people or to fix draining relationships. Financial worries can also be the result of misplaced priorities. Keep materialism in check by finding joy in your role as parent.

You can also find joy in simple things if you take responsibility for your own joyfulness. **Do not expect anyone else to give you joy. Go out and find it for yourself!** Finding joy is a habit. This habit starts with being thankful. Express thankfulness for everything positive you experience, do this every day. Do not rely on other people to give you happiness. Stop believing that having possessions will make you happy.

When you make decisions about how to spend time, let your life priorities be your guide. You and your child are a unit, a "we." You are no longer just an I. The question is not "How am I going to spend my time today?" It is "How are we going to spend our time today?" Your child does not require your undivided attention all the time. His need for you will be met if you include him in on most everything you do. You can then divide your time with your child between paying partial attention to him, and giving him your undivided attention. For example, keep your child with you while you do the household chores. **DO NOT PUT HIM IN THE OTHER ROOM IN A PLAYPEN WITH THE TV ON.** If you are in the kitchen, make a safe place for him to watch you. When you finish your work there, stop and take five or ten minutes to play with him. Then take him with you to do your next job.

When you reduce the stress in your life, adopt a joyful attitude, and keep your child with you as much as possible, you set the stage to have empathy and to be **responsive** to your child. Pay attention to your baby's needs. If he is not in your arms, he needs to be able to watch you and feel your presence. Attend to his comfort, try to get him on a predictable schedule, but be flexible. There may be times that he needs to eat more or less frequently, and sleep for longer or shorter time. After the newborn period, about 4 months of age, your baby also needs to play with you a little every day. If you have a "difficult baby" who cries a lot and is not easy to sooth, seek support from experienced mothers you know. Try to have friendships with more experienced moms. Perhaps an experienced mom can watch you with your child and help you try different strategies for soothing. Get into the habit of asking advice from more experienced parents. Just because they give you advice, doesn't mean you have to take it. If you do learn something that helps your child, you will be better off. Your child will also be better off if he has a number of adults that feel invested in his well-being.

Things You Can Do to Enhance Your Baby's Ability to Love

♥ Enjoy your little one!

♥ Keep him near you and **hold him often**.

♥ Be responsive to his needs for closeness and comfort.

♥ Smile at your baby often.

♥ Encourage your baby to smile at you.

♥ Play with your baby everyday, make him laugh.

♥ Talk to your baby; encourage him to respond to you.

Things that Impair a Baby's Ability to Love

■ Too little interaction with parents.

■ Caregivers who neglect his need for closeness.

■ Caregivers who neglect his need for comfort.

■ Caregivers who fail to smile and elicit joy from baby.

■ Caregivers who overwhelm baby.

Signs that the First Year Went Well

At the end of the first year, your child should be just about to walk and say a few words. He should laugh, make eye contact and play. He should also show a preference for the company of his mother and father.

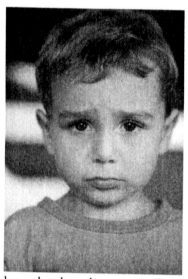

Fear and anxiety, if not excessive are good. Look for fear of strangers (stranger anxiety) in your child. This is a positive sign that will tell you that your child has learned to distinguish his immediate family as special. The fear response is important for **at risk** children[32] (see p. 124). Early signs of a fear response should be seen as a good indication your **at risk** child is developing normally. Separation anxiety is also positive. A child that becomes distressed at separation from his mother shows he has developed an attachment to her. **The quality of this attachment predicts how well the child will do for many years in the future.**

12-36 Months

The goal for the second year of life is to solidify and extend the enjoyment of attachment which began in the first year. Early in the second year, children become increasingly active in seeking positive support from parents.[33] It is important that you **respond** in a loving, positive way when your child reaches out to you for affection and companionship. Your child needs you now more than ever. Daily time spent in togetherness is the cornerstone of your relationship. Togetherness with a toddler can be tricky because toddlers also increasingly want to be independent and explore their world. Do not react to your child's growing independence by pulling away from him. He should not be permitted to use the rewards of independence as a substitute for the rewards of loving.

Sharing activities is one of the main ways humans bond with one another. Some children are so physically active that it is difficult to get them to slow down enough to appreciate quiet loving time.

A Match Made in Heaven?

Temperament is the "personality" your child was born with. Humans enter the world as unique individuals. Some babies are calm, others easily angered, some babies laugh a lot, others are more serious, some babies are curious, others are fearful. In families, there can be a temperamental mismatch between parent and child. It can be difficult for a parent to adapt to the temperament of his/her infant/toddler. Are you high-strung? If you tend to be nervous, a very busy active toddler may really test your patience. Are you busy, outgoing and sociable? If you are used to a lot of action in your life, then a high-strung child will have a hard time fitting in with you. One parent's easy kid is another parent's challenge. **A responsive parent adapts his/her lifestyle to suit the needs of his/her individual child.**

Responsiveness means meeting your child where he is. Perhaps, you will need to share some active loving time. I found that if I took my son on a long walk or played ball with him in the morning, he was then ready for some less active togetherness. It was difficult to get any of the housework done without attending first to his need for exercise. At the age of two, he was already capable of walking more than 2 miles!

I joked with my friends that my son was like a golden retriever, he had to have his daily exercise or all would suffer the consequences. I then searched the medical literature for studies using exercise to treat hyperactivity. Since some children are more physically active than others, it makes sense that these children (like some breeds of man's best friend) simply need more exercise. I was astounded at the lack of literature regarding the benefits of exercise in **at risk** children. I did find one well designed study that demonstrated that the hormonal response to exercise is blunted in unmedicated children with ADHD.[34] These children would indeed have to exercise much more to get that "adrenalin rush." The importance of the "adrenalin rush" may not be the rush itself but its after effects. The "adrenalin rush" may be needed to release other calming chemicals (pure speculation on my part). (After I wrote this, I found a book *Nature's Ritalin* by Stephen C. Putnam, it is about exercise and ADHD, this author agrees with my speculation.)

Toddlers benefit from more advanced play. Take your child to the park to play on the swings, teach him to throw and kick a ball. If the weather is cold, take advantage of an indoor play area. If you have a tendency toward depression, you will also find that forcing yourself to be active with your child will energize you and help you feel better. Once you have gotten your child to quiet a while, continue the habit of reading to him. Work puzzles together and play with blocks. Try to discover the things that interest your individual child. Having raised two girls and now a boy, I was amazed at the gender differences in interests. All three were interested in animals and music but my son was much more interested in motorcycles, trucks and trains than his sisters were. Responsiveness meant I too had to take an interest in motorcycles, trucks and trains.

The Terrible Twos

Is there any escaping the terrible twos? Whether or not your child is a difficult toddler has a lot to do with his temperament. However, research has shown that certain kinds of mothers have toddlers that listen more often.[35] The toddlers of these mothers are more likely to do what mom asks them to do and to stop when mom says "NO!" *What secret do these mothers possess?* These mothers simply held their babies more in the first year of life! ***Emotional warmth, especially as communicated through touch, promotes cooperativeness in the developing child.***

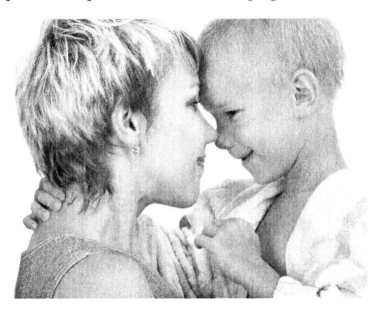

Your child's own capacity for empathy begins in the second year of life.[36] Empathy is our ability to sense the feelings of others and to respond appropriately to these feelings. Empathy therefore depends on understanding feelings, both in others and ourselves. Children must learn empathy through their relationships with their parents. Empathy is learned by teaching and example. When a toddler receives responsive empathetic care, he learns to associate caretaking with love.

Model, teach and influence, should become your favorite motto from now on. **Model** for your child the behavior you want to see in him. **Teach** your child with verbal lessons the things you want him to know. **Influence** him for the better with the tone you set.

A Parent's Pledge
Beginning today, I will be
A positive model for my child.
I will teach him to love.
I will be a positive influence,
Creating an atmosphere of peace
And joy in our home.

In the feeling realm, be a **model** for your child, demonstrate appropriate ways to express and cope with emotion. Try to be joyful as much as is naturally possible. Laugh when you feel happy. Do not be so reserved that you can't talk about sadness, anger or fear. **Model** sympathy and concern for others. Become your child's teacher. **Teach** him the words for feelings. Help him to recognize other people's reactions.

Picture books can be used to **teach** words for emotions, usually in these books, pictures of human facial expressions are included among other pictures. One day as we were looking at one of these books, my son pointed to the baby and said, "Baby crying." I then said, "Baby must be sad." A few weeks later, my son held an elephant squeaky toy. He said, "Elephant crying… it's O.K. elephant, don't cry." Through this kind of imaginative play, children make sense out of feelings and practice dealing with them. For the most part, a **responsive** caregiver can step back and just be an observer. Sometimes though, you may want to enter into the game, labeling feelings and modeling responses. The goal is for a child to know the words for and understand the basic emotions by around age three. If your child's speech is delayed, he may show you he understands the words even if he can't reliably say them.

Be a positive **influence** on your child's emotional development by providing a positive emotional climate for the family. Do not allow yourself to be angry or surly all the time. Too much anger and negativity in the home is particularly bad for the **at risk** child.[37] Do not create an atmosphere of distrust where your child wonders what kind of mood he will have to deal with today. No matter what your circumstance, try to find something to be thankful for, something to be positive about. You will find that your child will resonate with the emotional tone YOU set. **If you set a negative emotional tone, your child's natural sense of joy will be quenched.**[38]

Introduce your child to pets as early as is practical for your family. If you have a cat or a dog, **teach** your child to treat the animal lovingly. Let him share the chores of caring for the animal, providing food, water and exercise. My son enjoyed helping feed, water, and walk the dogs from the time he was 15 months old. Our neighbors driving by would slow down and smile at the sight of him walking one of our little dachshunds. That dog, herself a mother, thought of my son as a puppy. She gently walked ahead as he proudly held her leash. Everyone wondered just who was being walked! Sometimes children who have a hard time relating emotionally to people will relate to pets.

Another advantage of pets is they can be used to encourage the cute response. The "cute response" is the way we feel when we see something cute. It is a warm, fuzzy, pleasant feeling. I believe the cute response is innate in humans, but it needs to be nurtured and encouraged. Show your child pictures of human and animal babies. Respond to the pictures by saying "how cute" and smiling. Give your child many opportunities to connect with feeling affectionate. **Teach** him that affectionate feelings lead to caretaking.

Basic Feeling States Your Toddler Should Understand

As your child develops verbally, it is time for other important connections to form. Physical sensations accompany the basic human emotions–affection, joy, anger, sorrow, disgust, and fear. Have you ever felt your blood boil? Have you felt a lump in your throat or a sinking feeling in the pit of your stomach? Have you felt love in your heart? You want your child to connect these bodily sensations of emotion with the words for the emotion and the objects of the emotion. For example, affection for the dog is felt and verbally labeled as such, and connected to the mental image of the dog. **Responsiveness** means observing your child's readiness to make these connections.

Feeling	Signs of the feeling	What brings on the feeling?
Affection	Smiles, makes eye contact, hugs, kisses	Close family, pets, cute animals and baby humans
Joy	Smiles, laughter	Things I like
Sorrow	Tears, wailing	Pain and loss
Fear	Wide eyes, scream	Real or imagined danger
Anger	Frown, tone of voice	Things I don't like
Disgust	Scowl, "Yuck!"	Bad taste or smell

Responsiveness also means sensitivity in three other areas that may drive a wedge between you and your child. These areas are sleeping, feeding and toilet training. With all of these, your child needs to learn to respond to his own internal signals. Your goal is to lovingly help him to listen to himself. Of the three, battles over good sleeping habits are the most worth fighting. Children who tend toward impulsivity and hyperactivity are much worse when over tired. Help your child by sticking with a routine that allows for a set bedtime and nap. Some children can get their restorative nap in the car. Others will close their eyes for five minutes, and then be unable to nap the rest of the day. An evening spent with an emotional, impulsive, hyperactive toddler who didn't take a nap is most unpleasant. Fatigue and frustration in that situation may impair your ability to deal with your child in a loving way.

I also recommend you not try to force a child to eat food he finds repulsive or to eat more than his body tells him he should eat at any one time. Some children are naturally meal eaters while others are grazers. My son is a grazer. No matter what I tried, I could not get him to conform to the three meals a day plus snack life style. Instead, he ate smaller amounts every 2-3 hours during the day. I was relieved to read that some research shows eating small frequent meals actually leads to less obesity.[39] The important point is to try to understand your individual child. Studies demonstrate that the quality of attachment between mothers and young children is predicted by the mother's behavior around feeding her child.[40]

Regarding toilet training, I observed something very interesting when I read the literature. Many of the old books written 50+ years ago recommended starting toilet training around 14 months with the goal of completing toilet training by 24-30 months. This seems almost unheard of today. Many parents these days are inclined to wait until the child is fully ready before even starting training and that is now around 24 months. This approach is probably better than trying to force a child who is not ready. However, I wonder if this approach to toilet training doesn't reflect a larger shift in the behavior of parents in our society. Older books on child rearing also place a much greater emphasis on the importance of parents teaching children to control impulses than do the books of today. In the process of writing this book, I interviewed a number of women over 80 years of age regarding their observations of child rearing practices. It was universally noted that parents of today are more lenient and materially indulgent toward their children.

Things You Can Do to Enhance Your Toddler's Ability to Love

- ♥ Enjoy your toddler!
- ♥ Spend time daily with your toddler doing activities he likes.
- ♥ Model comfort with feelings.
- ♥ Teach words for basic emotions.
- ♥ Influence him with a positive attitude.
- ♥ Have him help care for pets and younger siblings.

Things that Impair a Toddler's Ability to Love

- ■ Too little interaction with parents.
- ■ Caregivers who are unresponsive to his needs.
- ■ Caregivers who are overly angry or anxious.
- ■ Caregivers who lack joy.
- ■ Caregivers who overwhelm the child with emotion.
- ■ Abuse in the name of discipline.
- ■ Trauma.

Love Ability and Day-Care

The danger placement in day-care with non-relatives poses to the development of a child's **ability to love** has more to do with the toll the day-care lifestyle takes on mothers than with day-care itself. Having been a working single mother myself, I have personal experience using both day-care and a nanny to help me care for my children. I can attest to the fact that life as a working parent with a child in day-care is no leisurely picnic in the park! The schedule is grueling. A mother with a child in day-care has to get up extra early to get that child and herself ready for the day.

She than commutes, drops the child off, works an eight or nine-hour day, picks the child up, and commutes again. By the time she gets home at 6 P.M. there is no dinner on the table. Luckily, the house is still clean because no one was there all day, but the laundry is not done. Emotionally, mother has to switch from the world of competing with adults to that of nurturing her child, and do this while fighting rush hour traffic. I just have one question. What kind of life is this for a mother and her child?

The challenge of maintaining the ability to be joyful and nurturing while living such a schedule is considerable. Meeting the challenge requires an extra effort at positive thinking. It also requires priorities. The child has to come first, and there may not be much room for anything or anyone else. Nurturing yourself must also be a priority. Friends and lovers of the single parent have to be a support. They have a moral obligation not to harm the already **at risk** child by upsetting his parent. It follows also that parents have to be a source of support to each other.

There is a difference between placement of a child in day-care with non-relatives, having a non-relative care for a child in his own home, and having a relative or close family friend care for a child. When a close family friend or a relative cares for a child, there is a sense of permanence to the relationship that does not exist with non-relatives. The sense of permanence makes for a more meaningful attachment to that caregiver. Nannies that care for children in the home often become part of the family, and relationships that form last a lifetime.

Working parents have to have an especially close relationship with their children when they are not working. Children who stay in their home with a parent have two advantages. The first is that because they spend so much time at home, they easily develop an emotional connection to "home." They feel safe and secure in their home. Children in day care have two homes. They only share one with their parent(s). There is therefore early development of a separate identity. In the best case scenario there is an emotional connection to two places, parent(s), and to the day-care staff. In the worst case, the day care arrangement pushes the child beyond his ability to attach and attachments to places and significant people are tenuous.

The second advantage children who stay at home with a parent have also involves time at home. It is easier for a parent to place himself in the center of a child's world if he is the child's world. The child's only choice is to interact with the parent at home because there isn't much else. If the parent is appropriately attentive, that child has an easier time attaching. The intellectual stimulation provided by day care can be very good for some children. For **at risk** children there will be a problem however, if the child prefers interacting with the stimulating environment to interacting with loved ones.

A well run community day care center can be a positive force in the lives of families if the entire family can form an attachment to the day care center. Some of these centers also offer parenting classes and parenting advice. A friend of mine who runs a community day-care center regularly tells me of former parents who call to give him updates about how their kids are doing, and to ask him about how to manage this and that childhood or adolescent problem. They call because they know the day-care staff still feel affection for their child and have knowledge and experience managing problems.

I raise the issues involved in day-care arrangements not to induce guilt or worry but to induce action. A child is small for a relatively short period of time. If a family has to make sacrifices for the sake of a small child, the sacrifices will be temporary. **It is not realistic to think that an at risk child can spend all day, five days a week in a substandard day-care, and the evenings with a tired, irritable, disengaged parent and still be O.K.** If you are a parent trying to make a day-care arrangement work, please be present for your child, physically and emotionally during the time he is not in day care.

Preschool, Ages 3-5

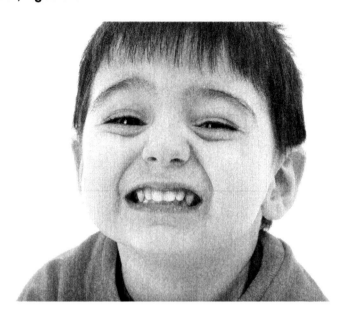

If your child has been at home rather than in day-care, now is the time to begin to introduce him to other children. The goal is to have him extend to others the affection he has developed toward his immediate family. He should enjoy the company of his peers. A finding I think is very interesting is that normally affection develops before aggression[41] (or competitiveness).

AFFECTION   **AGGRESSION**

Once developed, affection acts to lessen aggression children show toward one another. **The balance or lack of balance between affection and aggression is very important in the development of the ability to get along well with others.** A child who has affection for his peers will be motivated to keep his aggressive desires in check while he plays. If your child has the ability to extend affection toward his peers, he is ready for friendship.

Encourage your child to experience feelings of affection toward his friends, instead of spending all of playtime competing for toys and trying to best his friends in everything. **Model** affectionate friendships with your own friends. Influence your child for the better by valuing affectionate behavior over competitiveness.

Teach your child with your words about caring. Let your child hear you expressing concern and empathy for your friends and his friends. Be careful about how you criticize your own friends and your child's friends. A judgmental attitude does not **model** kindness. Have your child help serve his friends food and beverages when he hosts them in his home. "Guests go first!" is a good saying for the preschooler to learn. Encourage your child to be generous and to share his things. If a friend accidentally gets hurt during playtime, have your child help make him feel better. He can open the bandage package for the boo-boo. The point is to give your child as much opportunity as possible to learn affection and caretaking early on.

Influence your child with the tone you set during playtime in your home. Children will naturally compete with one another. This natural competitiveness can either be reduced or exaggerated by adult influence. For example, if your child seems to always want to show his superiority by running faster, jumping further, making the best drawing, painting the prettiest picture, having the nicest things etc. ask him to practice paying compliments to his friends. If you try to balance the competition by praising his playmate, your child may become even more competitive. Asking your child to acknowledge good in his friends will help get him in touch with his own affectionate feelings. If your child seems only to want to compete and to lack affectionate feelings, seek consultation with a professional about how to help him.

Try to monitor or have another adult monitor early play. Many child therapists recommend the use of play dates with structured activities children can share together. Avoid unsupervised situations where other children teach your **at risk** child unwanted behavior. For example, I worked very hard not to expose my son to hitting. I taught his sisters not to hit him no matter how annoying he became. Then one day, while he played with a group of children, one of the girls taught him the "hit me game." She would say, "Hit me! Hit me!" He would then hit her as they laughed together. In 10 minutes, two years of work went out the window!

It is now suggested that parents think of themselves as "coaches" when it comes to helping children with friends.[42] A good coach does not perform for the player. He teaches the player the rules of the game, observes his playing and helps him fine-tune his skills. The idea of parent as coach makes a lot of sense. We should not expect children automatically to know how to be a friend.

There are three areas where you can coach your child in friendship making. These are initiating activities and interactions, sharing and cooperation, and conflict resolution. Teach your child to greet others. Make play dates for him. When his friends are over, observe him. Teach him to share his things and show concern for the comfort of his friend. If conflicts develop gently intervene using the CPR method. (For more details, see *Preventive Parenting With Love Encouragement and Limits* by Thomas J. Dishion, Ph.D. and Scott G. Patterson.)

CPR stands for check, plan and review. Checking refers to understanding how each child involved views the conflict. Planning involves creating a positive resolution to the conflict. Reviewing means to review the plan with the child or children to make sure they understand it and carry it out. For example, two children are fighting over a toy. Check in with each of them to see why they are not sharing better. Help them make a plan to take turns. Review the plan and make sure they carry it out. If you find that much of the time during play dates is spent in conflict resolution, this is a sign that your child is overly focused on competitiveness and may need professional help.

A good nursery school is important for early socialization and may give you the first break you have had from your child since his birth. Look for a teacher child ratio of no more than 8:1. Once you have found a good nursery school, look to see how your child fits in with his peers. Avoid a situation where he is exposed to problem children. Do not put him in with other children who are overly competitive or aggressive. Choose peers with whom he can practice good social skills. It would be better to keep him home than to place him in a negative environment where unwanted inborn tendencies can become fully developed. Make sure adult supervisors have a plan for dealing with conflicts between children.

A good nursery school will prepare your child academically for school by teaching him his letters, numbers, colors and shapes. He will learn to write his name, and do arts and crafts. Emotional learning is also part of the nursery school curriculum. Teachers typically show children pictures of faces and ask what emotion is displayed. With the work you have done at home your child will indeed excel!

As your child gets older, the amount of time you spend physically holding him decreases. The relationship increasingly becomes dependent on shared experiences. A neighbor of mine told me of a practice his father began with him, that he continued with his own children. Every few weeks, he took one of his children out for an individual activity (he called it a date). Follow this example and make a habit of spending time with your children 1:1.

Today the day-care staff called a meeting with Jack's mom. Jack is a cute 3 year old but he is aggressive and overly competitive with his peers. His teacher became very alarmed when Jack spontaneously said, "my mommy hates me." Jack's mom came to the center looking sharp in her business suit, cell phone and Louis Vutton briefcase in hand. Annoyed and distracted, she asked, "What did you want to see me about?" The teacher answered, "We wanted to talk with you about Jack. He keeps repeating that you hate him." Appearing not to have heard the teacher, Jack's mom replied, "You should have seen the kind of day I had today, it was terrible..." The teacher interrupted her, "but Jack says you hate him." "Those clients are *just not nice people" was still the reply. The teacher tried to press, "Where would your son ever get the idea that you hate him?" But to no avail. Poor Jack, his mom just could not bring herself to focus on **his** needs.*

Things You Can Do to Enhance Your Preschooler's Ability to Love

- ♥ Enjoy your preschooler!
- ♥ Spend time daily with him doing activities he likes.
- ♥ **Model** comfort with feelings, and being a friend.
- ♥ **Teach** him to be caring, kind and affectionate.
- ♥ **Influence** him with a positive attitude.
- ♥ Become his friendship coach.
- ♥ Reward him for friendly rather than for competitive behavior.
- ♥ Have him help you care for pets and younger siblings.

Things that Impair a Preschooler's Ability to Love

- ■ Too little interaction with parents.
- ■ Caregivers who are unresponsive to his needs.
- ■ Caregivers who are angry, anxious and/or lack joy.
- ■ Abuse in the name of discipline.
- ■ Traumatic life events.
- ■ Excessive focus on competitiveness.

How to Repair Your Relationship with Your Preschooler

If your child is in pre-school and you are just now discovering that things haven't gone so well, don't despair that you didn't begin to work on the relationship sooner. Start today! Take inventory of the things that have reduced your ability to be **responsive** to your child. Again, draining adult relationships, financial worries, and misplaced priorities are the usual culprits. Resolve to reduce the stress in your life so you can be more emotionally available for your child.

Realize that you are the center of your child's life and he should love you intensely. Stop a moment to think about what it means to love. When you love romantically, don't you jump up every time the phone rings hoping it is that special someone? That is the way your child feels about you. He is elated when you show him attention and affection. Conversely, he is deeply disappointed at being neglected or ignored. Just as an adult is worn down by an emotionally unresponsive lover, so too is a child worn down by an emotionally unresponsive parent. **Do not give your child a reason to turn off.**

Renew your love on a daily basis. Make sure that every time you see your child following an absence you greet him cheerfully. Always kiss him goodbye and good night. Tell him he is special and that you love him. Prove your love by including him in your life. Keep him with you when you do chores and other life activities. Teach him to be your helper. Let him help you with chores. Then, take a few minutes each day, to give your child undivided attention. If your child has developed discipline problems that make him hard to be with, do not ignore him, address the problems (see Chapter 4). **Remember that we humans are creatures of habit. The habits that begin early tend to stick. Develop with your child a habit of loving.**

Houseplants

Very pleasing to the eye
Were all the houseplants I did Buy
Alas, too busy I did get,
I just could not, keep them wet
At my job I stayed all day
No time to water, no time to play.

When per chance I did look in
To see that foliage in the den
The plants had withered there
And in every room
Wilted, wasted, had they met their doom?

Terrified, I was just too late
I watered them hoping about their fate
Then, exhausted, asleep I fell
Not waiting to see if my plants did well
The very next morning when I passed by
My good fortune I cannot deny
Overnight my plants revived
No longer wilting, but looking alive!

Now I know what to expect
Wilting happens with neglect
But with a little, loving care,
Much, much better will they fare.

The Elementary School Years-More Shared Experiences

As I look back at grades K-5 with my daughters, I shed a little tear. The time went by so fast. We shared countless activities together, vacations, museums, hiking trips, days on the beach… the list goes on. In addition to these activities, there were nightly family dinners and of course the holidays. Interestingly, although both girls are bright, they do not remember all of the details of that time in their lives. However, what is important is that the relationship that resulted from all of the many enjoyable shared experiences remains solid. The shared activities formed the basis of a strong loving relationship; beautifully, the relationship endures even as the exact memories of the activities fade.

The elementary school years are critical for the development of thinking skills. The primary task of the school age child is to learn reading, writing and arithmetic. Since shared activities are crucial, it is important that you participate in your child's learning. Make sure he knows you are tracking his academic progress. Share books with him; spend time together with math flash cards. Teach him to tell time and use money. Do not rely solely on the school to teach your child.

During the elementary years, children begin to be involved in organized sports. Through exercise, your child can expend some of his physical energy while making friends and learning to play by the rules. If your child plays a sport, become his biggest fan. Go to his games and take pride in him. After the game, take him for a treat. If your child shows an interest in professional sports, connect with him by knowing the players on his team and cutting out newspaper articles about his team. The function of these shared moments is to build that solid relationship through mutual enjoyment. You want to be confident in the relationship you have with your child as he heads toward middle school and adolescence.

Be your child's biggest fan. No matter what activities he takes up, make it a point to watch and admire him. If your child is a dancer, go to the recitals. If your child plays music or sings, go to the concerts. Take as many photographs of your child as you can. Organize the photographs to albums, then, look at them with your child. Tell him you are very proud of him. Encourage your child to always do his best.

Friendships between children develop and deepen during the elementary years. Closely (but discretely), monitor your child's time with his friends. Look for signs of tenderness and reciprocity. How well does he share his things? Is he irritable and impatient? What tone does he use when speaking? Is he overly critical? Make sure the other children in your child's life are not cruel or lacking in empathy. Do not assume you have to put up with harmful influences just because they are in the neighborhood.

Research suggests that **at risk** children may be predisposed to pay too much attention to hostile cues from peers and not enough attention to positive cues. They tend to unnecessarily view peers as hostile.[43] Since they view peers as hostile, at risk children are likely to respond in kind. This return of perceived hostility only serves to evoke real hostility. Thus, **at risk** children become the masters of self-fulfilling prophecy.

The **model, teach, influence**, approach also applies to helping your child make friends during the elementary school years. Be careful not to **model** a style of judgmental suspicion towards others. Let your child see you giving people the benefit of the doubt. When possible, be complementary of other people's intentions. If your child tells you that other children are against him, ask for specifics. Help him to understand whether or not his own behavior may have been part of the problem. **Influence** him with optimism.

Be aware that your child may be listening when you talk with your friends either in person or on the telephone. Try to avoid any talk of people mistreating you. Treat your own friends with respect. Although you may feel that a suspicious or hostile style works for you, that approach may lead to problems for your child. Your child will imitate you. Raising your child properly may demand that you change your approach, or at least become very discrete.

Empathy–The Cornerstone of Ability to Love

Empathy is the ability to understand the world from another person's point of view AND motivation to treat another kindly based on that understanding. Some have suggested that motivation to treat another kindly happens because an empathetic person actually experiences another's feelings.[44] Individuals with antisocial personality disorder lack empathy. Those with addiction have impaired empathy, and children with ADHD have a difficult time developing empathy.[45] Other disordered people (narcissists), also completely lack the capacity to place themselves in another's shoes. It is interesting to observe that, those with antisocial personality disorder do have some ability to understand another's point of view. They are also very skilled at manipulation– the art of using this understanding for exploitation. **Empathy is the cornerstone of the ability to love, and therefore empathy is at the core of good**

character.

The development of empathy begins very early in life. The seeds for empathy are planted by **responsive** parenting during the infant-toddler period. Empathy then begins to grow during preschool. However, it is during the elementary school years that empathy either takes root and becomes a way of life or emotional callousness sets in. Empathetic teens really blossom and give joy to those around them. Teens that lack empathy are like thorny bushes– you try to avoid them.

One popular song says, "I feel sad when you're sad, I feel glad when you're glad, if you only knew what I'm going through, I just can't smile without you." This song describes what it is like to have empathy for a loved person. It also describes how your child feels about you. When parents express too much sadness (because of depression), or anger (because of poor **impulse control** and marital discord), children become overwhelmed. **At risk** children are particularly prone to becoming overwhelmed by a lot of emotion because they were not born with a good "control center" (see the next Chapter). Children that are overwhelmed are blocked from developing empathy. Since they can't cope with all those emotions, these children turn themselves off in order to survive.

Empathy starts with understanding feelings. Continue the habit of talking about feelings and discussing important matters with your child. I am not suggesting you make your child's life a perpetual therapy session (this would overwhelm him) just take advantage of opportunities as they arise. Studies show that children who can label and discuss feelings are better off.[46] Remember, comfort with feelings is learned behavior that might not come without effort.

Teach but Don't Overwhelm Your Child

It is important to talk about feelings as you observe them in your child and those around you. Whether or not your child becomes overwhelmed by his own or other people's feelings will depend on your attitude. If you panic when others show fear, sadness or anger, your child may do the same. A parental style that is overly dramatic confuses children. So, too much forced positive emotion is also not a good thing.

Your child shows he is overwhelmed when he turns off, loses control or breaks down. Provide comfort and reassurance to your child during times of high emotion. For example, if there is a death or illness in the family say "I am sad now, but I will be O.K., I just feel bad about..." If something really makes you mad say so, but show your child how to take the angry energy and turn it into something positive. "I am really mad that I lost my expensive earrings, I had better figure out how to be more organized with my stuff." If someone makes you angry, take the opportunity to model peaceful conflict resolution. If you and your child see another child in distress, either help the child or say, "he is sad, but he'll be O.K., he has _____ to help him."

Who will **teach** your child if you don't? Give your child feedback when you observe his emotions. "Seems like you really like being with Jimmy." "You were mad at me today when I asked you to clean up your mess." The basic feeling states your child should be able to recognize in himself and others are pain, fear, anger, surprise, jealousy, curiosity, affection, joy, self satisfaction, sorrow, guilt, shame and pride. Talk about the characters in movies, books and magazines; ask your child what he thinks about the character's feelings and motivations.

It is no accident that humans feel and express the set of feelings we do. An evening spent watching *Animal Planet* will likely show you that other mammals feel and express many of the same feelings. These feelings serve important survival functions. They also serve to promote togetherness and cohesion in social groups. Every feeling is associated with a set of stimuli or triggers, which elicit that feeling. That certain stimuli elicit certain feelings appears to be almost reflexive as if emotional responses are inborn. Remember that even inborn responses can either be strengthened or weakened by learning and experience (more on dealing with fear and anger in Chapter 4).

Human children learn about feelings by experiencing their own feelings. They also learn about feelings by watching and listening to other people. **What happens to emotional learning when children are visually or hearing-impaired?** Sensory impaired children are often delayed in the development of empathy. Impairment in the ability to recognize emotion occurs in visually and hearing-impaired children and adolescents. However, in hearing-impaired children, the impairment in emotional understanding is likely due to delayed verbal ability.[47] Verbal ability is very important in emotional control and processing. *Remember, words are powerful, use your words!*

The positive emotions are joy, affection, self satisfaction and curiosity. The degree to which we experience these positive emotions in our daily lives is to some extent within our control. Positive emotions come from positive self talk and an optimistic attitude. The positive emotions are also contagious, when we are around joyful and loving people, we are more likely to experience these emotions. **Teach** your child to practice positive self talk and to be joyful and affectionate. Help him practice self satisfaction by praising him for the good that he does. **Model** positive emotions and influence your family for the better. The following table gives a list of feelings you should **teach** your school age child about as opportunities arise in your daily life.

Feeling	Definition	Purpose
Joy	Response to pleasurable things	Self-preservation
Affection	Response to a loved person	Ensures family cohesion
Self satisfaction	Response to mastery of the environment	Motivation to do things
Curiosity	Response to novel stimuli	Ensures exploration
Fear	Response to perceived danger	Ensures physical safety
Surprise	Response to the unexpected	Signals the unexpected
Anger	Response to thwarting the basic drives	Signals frustration of drives
Jealousy	Response to having to share a loved person	Ensures competition for attention
Pain	Response to harmful things	Self=preservation
Guilt	Response to behaving contrary to moral standards	Essential for the survival of the group
Shame	Response to being low in social stature	Contributes to the stability of the social hierarchy

Clinical Depression in Mother or Father?

There are now many studies showing that children from families where there is too much sadness and/or anger have impaired ability to love. The right amount of joyfulness in the home nurtures children to develop empathy. Life with a clinically depressed parent can handicap a child. If you have depression, please get help. Thanks to medical science, there is now very effective treatment for depression. The right kind of help will reduce the level of your depression and teach you to live, even during times you are suffering. Never tell your child you are suicidal! Never let him over hear you talking of suicide! Parental suicide and talk of suicide can permanently damage a child.

What to Do if Your Ten-Year-Old Has Difficulty Reading Others

If your ten-year-old seems to have difficulty understanding and responding appropriately to other people's emotions, it is unlikely this is his only problem. Consider obtaining a psychological evaluation of your child. Children with ADHD can have difficulty recognizing the emotions of others.[48] Other **at risk** children show a selective impairment in ability to recognize sad and fearful facial expressions.[49] There are some activities you can do with your child to help him work on recognizing emotion. Take him to a local playground where younger children play. Take a note pad with you. Tell him that the two of you are going to play "scientist" for the day. Sit in a place where you can watch the other children. Use the above chart. Record and discuss instances where the children playing show emotion. Then at the end of your time, total up the number of observations you made. Talk about the feelings the two of saw. Ask your child how the experiment made him feel.

You can also watch soap operas on TV together with the sound turned off. Ask your child to guess about the emotions in the actors based on their gestures and facial expressions. If your child does not understand Spanish, you can watch Spanish language cable TV. Your child can then use cues from the tone of voice he hears as well as the people he sees. You can also play Charades. Ask your child to pantomime the emotions, see if you can guess them. Then pantomime them for your child and ask him to guess your emotion.

Laughter Is Good Medicine, But Teasing Is Toxic

Enjoyable time together is the key to strengthening relationships between parents and children. Children and adults alike, enjoy laughter. A child from a family that laughs together is less likely to feel that his circle of friends means more to him than his family. It is important to recognize though, that laughter should not come at a child's expense.

Children, even those that laugh at things being said, have low tolerance for being teased. Teasing is not pleasant for the one being teased. Adults that are at a loss for what to do or say often tease to release nervous energy. Adults who tease do not **model** empathy. Try to have a 'no tease rule' in your family. Defend your child from being teased by extended family members and other adults. Teasing by stepparents or the lovers of parents is especially bad for children. If the teasing occurs unchecked, in front of the parent, the child is left feeling vulnerable and alone. When a child feels vulnerable and alone, his natural response is to try to "toughen up." Some parents even tell children "you should have a thicker skin, and not be bothered by teasing." However, if a child "toughens up" or develops "thicker skin" his **ability to love** may decrease. Children often harbor deep resentment toward adults who tease them.

Excessive toughness leads to callousness and impairs the ability to love. However, a child who is overly sensitive also has difficulty with relationships. The overly sensitive child may perceive hostility where none is meant, and withdraws from peers and adults. Being a responsive parent means understanding your own child. An overly sensitive child should be encouraged not to view the social world as hostile. He should be encour-aged to give others the benefit of the doubt with regard to motives and comments. He should also be encouraged not to withdraw when injured, but to seek support. A child who is "tough" should be encouraged to "soften up" and enjoy the rewards of warmth and tenderness.

Things You Can Do to Enhance Your Child's Ability to Love

- ♥ Enjoy your child!
- ♥ Spend time daily with him doing activities he likes.
- ♥ Model empathetic behavior.
- ♥ Model comfort with feelings and people.
- ♥ Teach him about feelings.
- ♥ Influence him with a positive attitude.
- ♥ Continue to be his friendship coach.
- ♥ Encourage participation in music, sports and other meaningful activities.
- ♥ Become his biggest fan.
- ♥ Have him help you care for younger siblings.
- ♥ Have him care for pets under your supervision.

Things That Impair a Child's Ability to Love

- ■ Parental neglect.
- ■ Abuse in the name of discipline.
- ■ Traumatic life events.
- ■ Lack of comfort with feelings.
- ■ Excessive competitiveness.
- ■ Caregivers who are angry or anxious and lack joy.

- Adults who model suspiciousness and hostility.
- Peers that model callous behavior.

How to Repair Your Relationship with Your Child

If your child is in elementary school and you are just now discovering that you should have paid more attention to him sooner, do not despair. Start your lives together today! Take inventory of the things that have been more important to you than parenting your child. Draining adult relationships, financial worries, and misplaced priorities are the usual things that take parents away from caring for their children. Resolve to reduce the stress in your life so you can be more emotionally available for your child.

Realize that you are still the center of your child's life and he should still love you intensely. Stop a moment to think about what it means to love. When you love romantically, don't you jump up every time the phone rings hoping it is that special someone? That is the way your child should feel, or perhaps used to feel, about you. He should be elated when you show him attention and affection. He has been deeply disappointed at being neglected or ignored. Just as an adult is worn down by an emotionally unresponsive lover, so too has your child been worn down if you have been lacking in emotional responsiveness. **Stop giving your child reasons to turn off**. Renew your love on a daily basis. Make sure that every time you see your child following an absence you greet him cheerfully. Always kiss him goodbye and good night. Tell him he is special and that you love him. Prove your love by including him in your life. Keep him with you when you do chores and other life activities. Let him take pride in helping you with chores. Then take a few minutes each day, to give your child undivided attention. Make sure you attend all of your child's school events. Let him know you are his biggest fan. Special dates out are cherished by children. If your child has developed discipline problems that make him hard to be with, do not ignore him, address the problems. Remember, a solid loving relationship built during the early years will make the middle and high school years much easier.

Middle School

The peer group becomes increasingly important during the middle school years. At this time, children develop an intense awareness of themselves in relation to a human dominance hierarchy or pecking order. The social environment includes athletes, popular kids, nerds etc. It is apparent that "popular" kids are not necessarily well liked. "Popular" kids are at the top of the middle school pecking order. They are the ones the other children think "have it all." Generally, they are girls that are physically appealing and boys that are athletic and assertive.

Middle school kids are often brutal with one another and many seem to be lacking empathy. It is important for you to be involved enough with your son or daughter to hear about what is happening in the peer group. Try to help your child identify with the sufferings of other children. "Joe must have felt terrible when no one picked him to be on the team." "Mary must feel lonely and sad when the kids say she's weird." Help your child understand the concept of competition in the middle school pecking order. You have the perspective to know that traits that lead to social dominance in middle school are not necessarily those that lead to success in life. Emphasize that quality friendships do endure (maybe for life) if they are valued as more than a means to achieve social status. For example, your child's story can either be, "I'm glad I stuck by John even when the other kids made fun of him. He's been a great friend." Or, "That nice person I stopped being friends with because he wasn't "popular" enough, is now the Mayor."

Some schools are doing a fair job identifying and putting a stop to bullying. However, children engage in other behaviors that are hurtful but do not necessarily fall under the concept of bullying. I have observed that many parents feel proud of their children who are at the top of the middle school pecking order. They ignore the fact that their children get to the top in part by stepping on others. Middle school children whose parents **model** empathy are more kind and caring.[50] If your child tends to be "popular," **teach** him that leadership involves caring for those lower in status. Tell him it is his responsibility to model kindness.

The top of the middle school pecking order is a special problem for good looking **at risk** boys.[51] These boys can respond to the newly found social dominance in harmful ways, especially when their tendency toward affection and their tendency toward aggression are out of balance. For example, they can use their status to "get the girls" (sexually speaking). They can also develop a sense of entitlement or become self centered and grandiose (remember that being self centered and grandiose is a symptom of antisocial personality disorder). "Popular" boys desperately need to be taught the true meaning of greatness, friendship and leadership. Sometimes, when they are feeling their oats, these boys will not listen to a female adult. They need male role models that demonstrate good leadership qualities and the moral use of social power.

What Is a Sense of Entitlement?

A sense of entitlement is the belief that one deserves to be treated specially and receive favors from others. A child with a sense of entitlement has a hard time giving. He cannot allow someone else to go first. He attends to only his own needs, as he believes only his needs are important. A sense of entitlement underlies many disorders of character, and once developed during middle school, will last a lifetime. Therefore, do not allow your child to develop a sense of entitlement!

Many parents rightfully fear the *Brave New World* of middle school. A bad middle school peer environment has the potential to damage a child, even one who has had years of loving parenting. I have concluded that since middle school children are not capable of forming their own just society, they should not be permitted much unsupervised time. Make sure your child has well supervised social activities through sports, scouting, clubs and your spiritual community. Limit the amount of time your child spends playing without supervision with his friends in the neighborhood.

What about the fact that when we were kids our parents didn't supervise us that much? We said, "I'm going outside" and spent hours on our own with our friends. I am suggesting that unsupervised time is a recipe for disaster for the at risk middle school child. It must be remembered that **Love Ability** is still not fully developed in kids of this age. Experience can serve to strengthen **Love Ability** or to harden a child's heart.

Since the consequence of a middle school child being hardened to the pain and suffering of others may be the development of antisocial personality traits, it is self evident that violent media are detrimental.[52] Why should children be taught through video games or movies that people lying bleeding in the street is entertaining? Is this not horrific? All media the **at risk** child is exposed to should be closely monitored. There are two issues to consider. The first is the absolute dose of violence. The second is the context of the violence. For example, historical movies about prior wars may seem acceptable if they also carry a message about the horrors of war. Still, why should our children be exposed to violence on a daily basis? What good is it to teach a child to connect with that part of himself that is entertained by violence? **Why are we surprised when children who have been taught the entertainment value of violence, lack empathy, hurt each other and fight for the fun of it? We parents have created this problem in our vulnerable youth.**

Things You Can Do to Enhance Your Middle School Child's Ability to Love

- ♥ Enjoy your middle school child!
- ♥ Spend time with him doing things he likes.
- ♥ Celebrate special family time including meals together.

- ♥ Encourage friendships with peers who model good behavior.
- ♥ Continue to be his friendship coach.
- ♥ Be his biggest fan, take pride in his achievements.
- ♥ Give him responsibility for chores that help the family.
- ♥ Have him help you care for younger siblings.
- ♥ Have him care for pets under your supervision.

Things that Impair a Middle School Child's Ability to Love

- ■ Too little quality interaction with parents.
- ■ Abuse in the name of discipline.
- ■ Excessive drive for social dominance (Chapter 4).
- ■ A sense of entitlement.
- ■ Association with callous peers.
- ■ Exposure to violent entertainment.
- ■ Traumatic life events.

How to Repair Your Relationship with Your Middle School Child

Your child is in middle school and your relationship with him is distant and strained. YOU have to repair the relationship. How difficult it will be to repair the relationship depends on how early the relationship problems started. If the difficulties just started, they will be easier to address than if they began early on. If you have a long history of problems with your child, you will likely need professional help to fix your relationship.

Start by making your relationship with your child your top priority. Seek support from friends and family. Reduce outside sources of stress. Find common interests with your child. Share special time with him at least once a week. Continue with structured family time, especially nightly dinner together. When you can, show him physical affection, hugs and kisses. He may resist at first, but he'll get used to it! Make sure you are his biggest supporter and his biggest fan. Take an interest in how he is doing in school. Talk with him about his life.

If discipline has become a problem, address the problems (see Chapter 4). Stop criticizing your child. Criticism will not help him. It will only alienate him from you. If peer influences are harming your relationship with your child, put your foot down. Insist that he spend more time with you, even if he says he would rather be with his friends. Your child will start liking your time together once trust is restored. Trust cannot be restored without time together.

Why Is It Important to Have a Close Relationship with Your Middle School Child?

1)   Children have companionship needs; if your child doesn't get these needs met in his family he will likely hook up with other troubled kids. Association with troubled peers will damage your child.

2)   Your love relationship protects your child from the harmful effects of life stress.

3)   Your love relationship creates a conscience in your fearless child (Chapter 4).

4)   Your love relationship will give your child the skills he needs to care for your grandchildren!

Family Ties and Love Ability During the Teen Years

Your teen's friends are extremely important to his development. There are many studies showing that peer group behavior is a strong predictor of drug use, early sexual activity and criminal behavior during the teen years.[53] These studies do not necessarily address the fact that since "birds of a feather flock together" troubled teens seek each other out. Know your teen's friends. Make it clear that you expect your teen to select friends of good character.

It may seem that your teen does not enjoy family time. However, continue your habit of regular family activities, especially birthdays, holidays and vacations. Keep enjoying hobbies with your teen. Do everything you can to remain part of his life. No matter what his age, you will always be family. You owe one another allegiance. Your teen can express love and concern for his family by taking greater responsibility for household chores. It is important for a teen to feel his family needs his contribution. Keep in mind that until very recently in our history, the survival of a family did indeed depend on the work done by every member.

In addition to friendships, your teen will develop romantic relationships. If not properly managed, these relationships can be very destructive. **Teach** your teen that love involves responsibility for protecting the loved person. That means protecting the other from having feelings hurt in a relationship that ends. For example, a parent could ask a teen, "How would you feel if _____ became so obsessed with your relationship or upset by your break-up that his/her grades dropped and he/she couldn't go to his/her first choice college?" Most teens are not experienced enough to know the upset that relationships can cause. Discourage your son/daughter from early dating. Teens that begin dating around 14 generally have sex by 16. (See p. 141, for more on helping your child manage his sex drive.)

If you have a teenager you may have said, "Yeah right, easier said than done," when I spoke of discouraging early dating. The key to keeping focus in your teen's life is to **teach** him to value doing well in school, participating in meaningful activities, and having quality friendships. Teens who study, have meaningful activities and good friends don't have enough free time or energy to become obsessed with a girl or boy friend.

It is also important to **teach** those approaching adulthood caring beyond friends and family. Take charge of teaching your teen concern for others and the greater community. Encourage a life habit of community service. Look at your yearly calendar and set dates for volunteering together. Select activities that go with different holidays:

If you do community service monthly, that is only twelve times a year. If your teen plays a musical instrument, arrange for him to play in a nursing home on a regular basis. If he likes animals, he can volunteer in an animal shelter. Encourage your teen and his friends to do a yearly walk or run for charity. I found that community service is a good vehicle to expose teens to spiritual communities outside their own. One of my daughter's friends regularly volunteers at a church sponsored soup kitchen. By volunteering with her friend, my daughter was able to learn about her friends faith. The two of them

MONTH	HOLIDAY	PROJECT
January	Martin Luther King Day	Urban renewal project
February	Valentine's Day, Veterans Day, President's Day	Soup kitchen, civic project, place flowers on graves of Veterans
March	First day of spring	Clean up a local park, plant a tree, walk or run for charity
April	Easter/Passover, Arbor Day, Earth day	Project in place of worship, Plant a tree, clean up a park
May	Mother's Day, Memorial Day	Visit nursing home, honor veterans, visit senior neighbor with no local family, adopt a grandma
June	Father's Day, Flag Day	Visit a nursing home, visit senior neighbor with no local family, adopt a grandpa, honor the flag
July	Independence Day	Civic project, write a letter to a soldier
August	Vacation, Jewish High Holidays	Raise money for a charity, volunteer at the local library, help a younger neighbor child practice reading and math skills
September	Labor Day	Urban renewal project
October	Columbus Day	Celebrate new immigrants by eating out at an ethnic restaurant, rake leaves for a neighbor who needs help
November	Thanksgiving	Volunteer at food bank, collect winter clothing for homeless, work at a soup kitchen
December	Christmas, Chanukah	Toys for Tots

found caring for the poor to be a value shared by people of many different faiths. After school youth groups also can provide young teens with opportunities to volunteer and contribute to the community.

Things You Can Do to Enhance Your Teen's Ability to Love

- ♥ Enjoy your teen!
- ♥ Be his biggest fan, take pride in his achievements.
- ♥ Spend time with your teen doing activities you both enjoy.
- ♥ Celebrate special family time, including meals together.
- ♥ Expect your teen to help run the household (this is how he expresses caring).
- ♥ Give your teen opportunity to care for younger siblings.
- ♥ Give your teen the responsibility of caring for pets.
- ♥ Encourage friendships with peers that model good behavior.
- ♥ Encourage community service.

Things that Impair a Teen's Ability to Love

- ■ Too little quality interaction with parents and other adults.
- ■ An excessive drive for social dominance.
- ■ Association with callous peers.
- ■ Enjoyment of violent entertainment.
- ■ Sexual promiscuity, substance abuse.

- Traumatic life events.
- Abuse in the name of discipline.

How to Repair Your Relationship with Your Teen

Repairing a broken relationship with a teen is much more difficult than repairing a relationship with a younger child. Problems have had a longer time to take root, and sometimes the roots are very deep. Dangerous acting out by your teen has to stop before relationship repair can begin. Dangerous acting out can include violent behavior, running away, sexual promiscuity and drug use. If your 14 or 15 year old is already doing these things, realize that you are now in the realm of secondary prevention of antisocial behavior (see p. 10) and you need professional consultation.

Start again by making a list of your teen's strengths and good qualities. Let a vision of these guide you as you seek to reform your teen's life and your relationship with him. Address discipline with contracts and consequences (see Chapter 4). The use of contracts and consequences will lessen conflict between you and your teen. Stop with the guilt trips and criticism, they don't work, and will drive a wedge between you and your teen.

Find enjoyable activities that you and your teen can share together. Give your teen hugs and physical affection when you can. He may not act as if he enjoys this at first, but he will over time as your relationship improves. Limit the amount of time your teen has to "hang out" with friends. When parents neglect a teen's emotional needs, the teen seeks to have these needs met with peers. Stop this vicious cycle by spending lots of time with your teen. If you cannot be there for him, find other adults that will help you with him. Get him involved in supervised, structured activities, like team sports and youth groups.

Give your teen lots of positive feedback for the good things he does. Give him a chance to earn trust by assigning him jobs to do in the house and around the yard. Avoid power struggles by clearly and consistently asserting your authority, not by giving into his demands. Do not expect immediate results. It can sometimes take months of working on a more positive relationship to chip away at the walls that have been built up.

Keeping the Lines of Communication Open

While sharing activities is important, sharing thoughts, feelings and ideas is also important. Keeping the lines of communication open involves listening and speaking. When your child or teen indicates he wants to chat, show him you are interested by facing him and listening. Get him to talk more by asking questions. Sometimes you can encourage a reluctant child to talk by making jokes or saying something shocking in jest. What ever you do, do not use intimate talking time to sit in as judge and jury. Take mental notes of the things your child tells you that may be alarming. Plan to address problems later, do not over react or criticize. Emotional reactions and criticism will make your child reluctant to share himself with you.

It has been my observation that children love it when their parents talk about themselves and their own childhood. Be choosey about what you share, for example do not tell your child too much about the bad things you did when you were his age. But, do talk about your own experiences and feelings as a child. Disclose yourself in a way that will tell your child that you remember what it is like to be a kid. Be selective, but talk about your own hopes and dreams.

A walk or a ride in the car can sometimes be used to get a child to talk. If I suspect there is something one of the girls wants to tell me but is reluctant, I initiate a walk or a ride in the car. Then I put on my listening ears. I ask general questions, and make light of things. If you can get your child talking by asking him about things that he likes to talk about, the conversation will naturally drift to the other things that are on his mind. (Psychiatrists and psychologists learn this "trick" as part of their training.) The goal is to be perceived as interested, empathetic and non-judgmental. If communication has become very difficult due to "bad blood," you may have to have a number of walks or rides in the car before your child will disclose what is really on his mind.

Guiding Your Child in the Midst of Tragedy

There is no doubt that trauma can harden a child and impair his **ability to love**. There are many studies showing that stressful life events can undo some of the positive effects of good early attachment.[54] Family tragedy is unavoidable. Death, divorce, sickness and job loss happen in life. If you come from an "at risk" background, you will likely experience more than your share of adverse life events. I cannot sugar coat the situation. Trauma is damaging to children (and adults for that matter), the body's hormonal response to trauma actually changes the structure of the brain.[55] Emotional pain is also harmful because it causes distraction from the job of personal and educational growth. Therefore, when disaster strikes, children need the kind of help that reduces the physical response to stress and allows them to continue developing through the pain.[56]

First, keep your child on a steady schedule; disrupt his routine as little as possible. Make sure he eats properly and gets enough sleep. Insist he continue to focus on personal growth and academics. He will likely find that time spent studying or in activities will distract him from his pain. Using constructive activities to distract from pain is a mature way to cope– not a bad life lesson to learn. Continue in sports, clubs and religious observance as much as possible.

Maintain a close relationship with your child and work for family unity. Love relationships act to dampen the body's hormonal response to stress,[57] so your relationship with your child can actually protect him from the harmful effects of trauma. If your child feels close to you, he will also be more likely to talk about how he feels. Give your child a chance to talk about the trauma and work through his sense of grief. Let him speak his mind even if it is painful for you.

Getting through a tragedy can be a growth experience for

everyone in the family. You **teach** your child to cope with tragedy by talking to him about how to make the best of a bad situation. Be a good example by **modeling** coping strategies yourself. Grieve, but do not stop living. Make sure you take time out for regular recreation together.

When my son's father was arrested, my son was only four months old. However, my daughters were 10 and 12. I was devastated and filled with shame over the pain the experience caused the girls. The pain was magnified by the fact that his arrest lead to the loss of my job and status in our community. Today the girls, 13 and 15 are A students, have a wide range of interests, good friends and are thriving. They continued to develop emotionally, socially, and academically through the trauma. There is also a stronger sense of family and togetherness now than ever before.

Getting my family through this tragedy required a total personal commitment. I am not one to glorify a horrible situation. Although they matured through the experience, the girls would have been better off if they had not had to suffer. That being said, what did I do to reduce the effects of the trauma on the girls?

First, I kept their schedules the same. We stuck with regular meals together and a set sleep time. They were not allowed to miss school or other prior commitments. I telephoned our friends, explained the situation and was blessed by many parents who had the girls over for play dates and sleep-overs. We continued to go to religious services regularly– even though I didn't exactly feel like showing my face in public. The needs of the children had to come first. We celebrated holidays and birthdays with more gusto and renewed appreciation. I told the girls verbally and through my actions that we were going to make it and their lives would be good.

Because of my unemployment, our financial resources were very limited. Nevertheless, we did things together that did not require money. We went camping during vacations; the trips cost very little and fostered much togetherness. We also learned a lot, and gained a sense of peace that comes with being in nature.

Getting the family mobilized in the midst of such stress required that I reach within myself and to God. From the inner and outer resources, I found the strength to continue to parent the children and lead the family. Due to their grief, the girls resisted many of my efforts to keep their lives going forward. Their resistance took a real toll on me and required that I remain steadfast in my convictions. For example, when my older daughter found out we were going camping, she cried. She interpreted the camping trip as confirmation that indeed we would never be able to stay in a hotel again. We talked about her fears; I reassured her that I was committed to giving our family a good life. "No, we don't have money now, but let's make the best of our situation." She still was not enthusiastic about camping. I had to be excited enough for both of us. My reward came the first night during a rainstorm. The girls were in their tent with flashlights on laughing and playing cards together. It was only at that moment that I was absolutely sure I had done the right thing. Then, while alone, I cried.

If I had allowed the trauma and my circumstances to get the better of me, I would not have been able to care for my precious children. My son needed all my love and the girls needed me to give them a clear message. "I am in charge here." "No matter what, you have a mother who loves you and makes your needs a top priority." *Unfortunately dear ones, you will face hard times in life. The way you cope will define you as a person.*

Mother and Father

"You go to war with the army you have, not the army you want." –Donald Rumsfeld, Secretary of Defense.

Experts are unanimous in the conclusion that it takes two loving parents in the home to optimally raise a child. That being said, the optimal situation is not available for many of America's children. We are left with having to strengthen the "army" of parents we have. I use the military analogy to make another important point. Even those who disagree with the war, still have to support the troops!

Just as we have to do everything possible to avoid war, we have to do everything possible to avoid single parenthood. Once, war (or single parenthood) is declared, we have to fight to win! Single parents need all the love and encouragement we can give them. Most have plenty of guilt over their situation. The consequences of losing with our children are misery, crime and addiction.

What about father? Is attachment to father the same as attachment to mother? How does the importance of father change with the age of the child? Is father especially important for **at risk** children? Can a man be mother? We don't have firm answers to all of these questions. Studies do support the idea that attachment to father is not the same as attachment to mother. Children do not necessarily generalize their relationship with their mother to their father.[58] The father-child relationship has to hold its own. Therefore, all of the guidelines I have given regarding holding of infants and shared enjoyable activities with older children apply to father as well as mother. If father wants to count, he has to work at having a relationship with his child. He cannot rely on mother to do the "family thing" for him.

In two parent families where the male partner stays home and cares for the kids and the female partner is in the work force, the female partner is usually still mother. Generally speaking, the woman remains the primary attachment figure. That doesn't mean that in a single parent situation, a man can't function as mother. Single fathers (like single mothers) should focus on **responsiveness**. Be sensitive to the feelings and needs of your child, expressed and unexpressed. If the single father is slightly disadvantaged (by biology) when it comes to **responsiveness** he should also be at an advantage when it comes to training **impulse control**. A weak single mother in the area of training **impulse control** may have a worse outcome than a slightly less **responsive** single father (see Chapter 4).

An impaired mother or father can also be a negative force in a child's life.[59] In families where there is one mentally healthy parent and one impaired parent, the healthy parent also has to care for the dysfunctional partner. Caring for the dysfunctional partner takes time and energy away from caring for children. This problem is especially tragic when the dysfunctional parent refuses to make better choices and is abusive.

I would argue that in cases where the dysfunctional partner repeatedly refuses to get help or follow professional advice, children are better off with only one parent. There are studies that support this position. If you are in the very difficult position of choosing between saving your child and trying to save your dysfunctional partner, I would suggest the following: If your child is still small, you have a great likelihood of raising him to be a healthy adult. You may not be as lucky when it comes to saving your partner. For older children, being constantly vexed by an angry, abusive or addicted parent is very bad. In most cases, it makes sense to opt to save your child.

CHAPTER 4

IMPULSE CONTROL– ALWAYS A WORK IN PROGRESS

What Are Impulses?

An impulse is a thought to do something. Impulses come from our basic drives and emotions. Our basic drives are for the things that give us pleasure: nourishment and comfort, physical and emotional contact with other people, sexuality, social dominance, and entertainment. (If you doubt that entertainment is a basic drive, just think about how much money you spend on it each year!) **Drives and emotions lead to impulses or thoughts to do things.**

What are Drives?

What exactly is a drive? A drive is a very powerful force within us that makes us want to do something. Furthermore, when we do what our drives tell us to do we are rewarded with pleasure. It makes us feel good to act in accordance with our drives. The problem is that we have a hard time doing enough to satisfy all of our drives. Take for example, the drive to eat. Most people who allow their appetite to tell them what food to eat and how much to eat, become over-weight. This is why so many people are obese. While our brains have well developed systems to tell us what to do ("GO!"), the systems that tell us "STOP!" do not function as well. This is true for ALL of the basic drives. Learning how to activate the "STOP!" button is very important. **This learning should begin as soon as the drives begin (around age 2).**

What Is Impulse Control?

When we speak of **impulse control**, we are really talking about controlling our reactions to the impulses that come from our basic drives and emotions. A person with a lot of **impulse control** or will power can resist his drives and control his actions. Strong **impulse control** or will power protects against ADHD, addiction and antisocial personality disorder. Impulsivity is the opposite of **impulse control**. Impulsivity has also been defined as "A predisposition toward rapid, unplanned, reactions without regard to the negative consequences of these reactions."[60] Impulsive people are quick to do things. They do not take enough time to plan or consider the consequences of their actions. Impulsivity is an important symptom of ADHD, addiction and antisocial personality disorder.

Impulses are filtered through an "impulse control center." The impulse control center determines which impulses are acted upon. The impulse control center also acts to suppress impulses. A person with a defective *impulse control* center has both more impulses and decreased ability to control his actions.

Unwanted actions can result from very strong drives and emotions. The strength of these overwhelms the impulse control center. Unwanted actions can also result from a weak impulse control center. In either case, poor **impulse control** leads to the inability to "STOP!" and delay gratification of the basic drives. Remember, all behavior is determined by our basic drives and emotions.

What does science tell us about the basic drives and the impulse control center? The ability to delay gratification of the basic drives ("STOP!") and therefore to control impulses, is directly related to the amount of inhibition in the brain. Injury to, or impairment of the front part of the brain, reduces inhibition, damages the impulse control center, and impairs **impulse control**.[61]

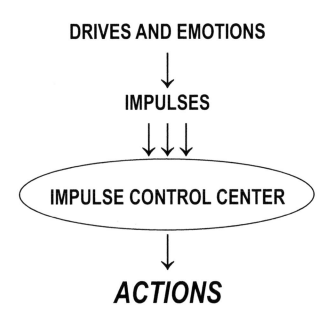

DRIVES AND EMOTIONS

↓

IMPULSES

↓ ↓ ↓

IMPULSE CONTROL CENTER

↓

ACTIONS

Think about the way the human brain is shaped in comparison to that of other mammals. A major difference is in the front part of the brain, which is relatively very large in humans. This large front part of the brain makes it possible for humans to exert control over impulses to a far greater degree than other mammals do. When a parent imparts **impulse control**, he is actually strengthening the structure of his child's brain! This strengthened brain structure serves to protect the child from dangerous impulses. For example, without **impulse control**, children would be cut by knives, burned by fire, hit by cars and injured falling off high places. **Strong inhibition is also required to protect against antisocial personality disorder, addiction and ADHD.**

Just as for any other physical trait, the amount of inhibition present in the brain varies among individuals. Genes influence the nature of the physical traits an individual possess. Some children easily develop **impulse control.** A child who easily develops impulse control does so because he was born with a strong impulse control center. The front part of his brain has plenty of inhibition. Generally speaking, **at risk** children are more impulsive. They have a more difficult time controlling their behavior. We have to assume though that the right kind of parenting can increase the amount of **impulse control** a child has. The opposite is also true, inadequate parenting is a cause of poor **impulse control**. With any particular child, it is difficult to tell if poor **impulse control** was inborn or is related to inadequate parenting.

Remember, there are likely critical periods in development that limit the degree to which **impulse control** can be learned at a given age. The goal is to work with your child according to his own ability. Encourage your child to do the best he can, but do not despair if your school-aged child is impulsive. Instead, make a plan (perhaps with professional help) to work on behavior.

Do You Have a Strong-Willed Child?

Many books have been written about the so-called "strong-willed" child. These books generally present very good advice about limit setting with difficult children. By most accounts, a strong-willed child is one who does what ever he wants and opposes adult correction. Strong-willed children also have poor control over their own impulses.

The concept of the strong-willed child is confusing because it implies a child with good will power. Will power, or impulse control, enables children to focus on school, work and meaningful hobbies. Will power helps children behave in a good way and resist temptation. Will power developed over the course of childhood protects against ADHD, addiction and antisocial personality disorder. The so-called "strong-willed child" actually has poor will power, NOT good will power!

But, the concept of the strong-willed child makes so

much sense, what is really going on? Instead of having will power, strong-willed children have an out of control drive for social dominance (see p. 127). The drive for social dominance makes them resistant to correction because they always want to be "in charge." Thus, they only appear to be strong-willed.

Why am I quibbling over words here? The reason is this: it is important for parents to recognize that the source of oppositional behavior in children is BOTH poor impulse control AND a strong social dominance drive. These two things often go together in **at risk** children. A parent of an **at risk** child has to overcome the strong social dominance drive while teaching impulse control. THIS IS NOT AN EASY TASK!

Training Impulse Control

Impulse control is a habit. This habit changes brain structure. I am suggesting you work on developing in your child a habit of control over the expression of the basic drives and emotions. *If you train up a child in the way he should go, even when he is old he will not depart from it.*[63]

The **model**, **teach**, **influence** approach is critical for the building of **impulse control**. How can you expect your child to have **impulse control** without you as a **model**? To be effective, a parent must **model impulse control**. You must also **teach** your child all the important life habits. A good teacher gives attention and praise for positive efforts, and ignores or sets limits on negative behavior. You must **influence** your child by placing a value on **impulse control**. Note that what I am calling impulse control is commonly called self-control. I choose not to use the term "self control" because 1) impulse control is more precise and 2) because (hopefully) the Self is defined as much more than a bunch of impulses. The use of the term "impulse" allows us to identify a good Self in even the most impulsive child.

Regarding modeling, teaching, and influencing **impulse control**, one respected author states, "When parents fail to take this responsibility, the social development of their children is left to chance."[64] I would reframe this to say that when parents are distant and under-involved, the development of children is left to genetics and biology, not chance. **Without positive parenting, there is no possibility of shaping development beyond the narrow framework of genetic endowment.**

Slow Down and Smell The Roses!

Some scientists believe that poor impulse control happens because children are too quick to do things. A child in hyper-drive acts before he thinks. Help your child by gently encouraging him to SLOW DOWN.

Teaching Impulse Control to Preverbal Infants and Toddlers

Before a child can understand and use words, he has only two tools at his disposal for **impulse control**. **Redirection** and **distraction** are really the only defenses against impulses a preverbal child has. Redirection is the creation of an appropriate setting for the expression of impulses. Distraction is the process by which attention shifts away from undesirable impulses.

Children learn redirection and distraction spontaneously and through teaching. Studies show that the most effective parents **teach** distraction and redirection to help preverbal children begin learning **impulse control** early.[65] Say your child persistently wants to entertain himself by playing with your car keys or cell phone. Well, the problem is that your keys get lost and your cell phone gets broken. A **responsive** parent would provide his child with substitutes for these, fake keys and a plastic phone. By providing your child with substitutes, you acknowledge his desires as legitimate, set limits and **teach** him to direct himself in a way that is productive rather than destructive. Other parents set aside special kitchen drawers for a toddler to explore.

Distraction can also be used to help a preverbal child cope with emotion. Many parents distract a crying child by cuddling him and making funny faces. In this exercise, the child learns to shift attention from a negative feeling state to a more positive one. **Practice redirection and distraction as much as you can with your child.**

When problems arise, ask yourself, "How can I distract my child?" and "How can I redirect his behavior toward a better activity?"

As soon as your child acquires language, words become the primary means of strengthening **impulse control**. It is fascinating to watch a toddler struggling to use words to control his impulses. The process is not unlike that by which children learn to ride a bicycle. The first efforts are very deliberate and require a great deal of effort. Then with practice, the process becomes automatic. Watch as your child picks up the previously mentioned keys or cell phone while repeating to himself "don't touch mommy's keys" and "don't play with mommy's cell phone." Commanding himself to put the objects down requires a great deal of effort. You may also notice that the commands your child gives himself are identical to the ones you have given him. Your words are remembered. **Your child then uses your words to build his own impulse control center.** If you have witnessed this process, you have observed the building blocks of conscience (more on conscience later). Once the conscience is fully formed, the process of verbal command over impulses happens automatically. The child can stop himself without thinking about it.

Words are powerful. Use your words! Is a favorite saying of my friend who runs a day-care center. Children need to be taught to use their words both to control their own impulses and to influence the behavior of others. **Teach** your child that instead of just taking a toy back from a classmate, he should ask him for it. If someone hits, do not hit back, tell an adult. **Teach** him to talk about conflicts, and to try to resolve them through verbal rather than physical means.

Teaching Impulse Control by Using Rewards and Setting Limits

You **teach impulse control** when you use rewards and set limits on your child's behavior. When teaching **impulse control**, remember children learn best when there are clear rules and clear consequences. Establish clear rules for behavior in your home (see below for examples) and out of your home. Enforce the rules consistently. By establishing clear rules and enforcing them consistently, you cut down on the number of challenges to your authority (see p. 133).

Some rules for school work:

Turn in all notice papers your teacher gives you
Do your homework before play
Keep your notebooks neat and organized
Tell parents about any large homework projects; do not
wait until the last minute
Always turn in your best work
Study for tests, read the textbook

Some rules for nice behavior:

Do not grab objects from other people
Share things
Do not yell at anyone, No foul language
No hitting
Do not enter another's space without knocking
Help with chores, according to your ability
Use other good manners

Some rules for behavior at home:

No running in the living room
No yelling in the house
No eating outside the kitchen and eating areas
Finish playing in time to put away your toys
Pick up after yourself in the bathroom
Put your dirty clothes in the hamper
Put trash in the garbage can
Do not touch the papers on mom's and dad's desk

Some rules for personal hygiene:

Wash your hands after using the toilet and playing
outside
Wash before eating
Take a bath every day
Brush your teeth in the morning and before bed
Attend to your appearance, wear clean clothes
Comb your hair

Practice Positive Parenting

Positive parenting means shaping your child's behavior with rewards instead of just responding to what he does. It is easy to get into negative parenting habits when it comes to dealing with **at risk** children with poor **impulse control**. The impulsive behaviors of these children make life very difficult for parents. Finishing activities such as cleaning and shopping can be next to impossible as the child gets into trouble as his parent tries to get things done.

How should parents protect **at risk** children from entering into situations they cannot handle? The answer is different for every child but in general if you frequently become angry with your child in a particular circumstance, avoid that circumstance and consider changing your expectations. If your child repeatedly makes the same mistake, perhaps your lifestyle has demanded more of him than he has the maturity to cope with. For example, if your child has many, toys in his room, he will make an enormous mess there every time he is left alone to play. He is not willing or able to clean up the mess. It is up to you to organize his things and to limit the number of toys he has so he won't make more of a mess than he can clean up. Similarly, when eating out at restaurants or shopping be sure not to linger too long. Avoid situations that provoke you to feel ill will toward your child.

How can a parent use rewards wisely? **At risk** children need immediate, positive feedback for good behavior. If your child is having a difficult time establishing good life habits, you may need to more closely supervise him and reward him for each little job well done. The use of stickers on a check off list or tokens placed in a piggy bank can be used to encourage children to do what is expected of them.

It is also important to know when NOT to give a reward. Do not reward your child for doing anything he already enjoys doing. The doing of the activity is a reward in and of itself. For example, *if* your child enjoys reading do not reward him for each book read. A reward under these circumstances may actually reduce the amount of reading he does because your child will attribute his reading to the reward rather than to his own enjoyment. Similarly, children who enjoy music actually practice *less* when rewarded for practicing. The best reward for children who are doing good things and enjoying themselves is to express pride in their good character.

Use rewards to establish life habits in activities your child cuts corners with. For example, your child's morning routine may involve several steps. He must get out of bed on time, wash up, comb his hair, brush his teeth, dress, gather his belongings and eat breakfast. If you find yourself frazzled every morning because your child can't get into a good routine, make a written list of the things you want your child to do. When he does each job, put a sticker next to that item on the list. At the end of the week, have your child trade in his stickers for a larger reward. Use this system to help your child develop good habits with his chores and homework. Make lists of the tasks required to complete a given job. After you make the list, verbally explain it to your child, or let him help you make the list. Then you can be sure your child understands what is expected of him. The **at risk** child needs rules and expectations clearly spelled out. You will find that it is more pleasant to reward your child's good behavior than to set limits on your child's impulsive behavior. Catch your child in the act of doing good things.

Rewards that encourage good behavior:

Verbal Praise
Verbal Praise with a hug
Ribbon, badge or certificate
Increase in privilege

Money
Toy
Meal or treat out at a restaurant
Trip to the movie theater or other local attraction

A Trip to Wal-Mart

One evening over the holiday season, we happened to make a trip to Wal-Mart. Everyone there was in a hurry, trying to make his or her last minute Christmas purchases. We entered the store along side a mother with a 10-year-old girl who was whining. Suddenly, the mother slapped her daughter's face stating; "Don't you ever talk to me like that!" The screams of that child were then heard throughout the store. I question whether anything we parents do is really that important. If we are stressed and pressured, why not take a break and stay home?

Positive parenting means protecting a child from entering into situations he won't be able to handle.

Five Steps to Limit Setting

Even when parents work hard to establish good life habits, children still need to be corrected for misbehavior. **The purpose of correcting misbehavior is to teach impulse control.** Correction of misbehavior for the purposes **of teaching impulse control is called** *limit setting.* Limit setting is not the same as punishment because punishment does not necessarily **teach impulse control.** When you see misbehavior occurring or about to occur, there are five basic steps to limit setting:

1) Get your child's attention.
2) State the rule.
3) State the correct action or give a reason.
4) Give a warning or consequence.
5) ALWAYS follow through with consequences.

Get your child's attention.

Getting your **at risk** child's attention may not be easy. A child engaged in an activity may try to ignore you. Sometimes it is necessary to stop your child, hold his arm and look him right in the eyes as you state a rule.

State the rule.

Your rules should be short and simple. When you state rules, do so in a matter of fact tone, with few words. You want the rules to sink in. It is easier for your child to remember short simple statements.

State the correct action or give a reason.

Connecting correct actions and reasons to rules helps your child to develop **moral reasoning ability** (see Chapter 5). Again, don't be long winded or give complicated explanations. Keep your instructions simple.

Give a warning or consequence.

Consequences should be simple and immediate.[66] Consequences imposed by parents for undesirable behavior should directly relate to the undesirable behavior. For example, a child who refuses to do his chores in a timely fashion faces the consequence of not being allowed to go out and play. Consequences should be proportional to the misdeed– small consequences for minor infractions and large consequences for really dangerous behavior.

Always follow through with consequences.

If you do not always follow through, your child will ignore your warnings and constantly test you. Cut down on hassle for yourself, always follow through and DO NOT NEGOTIATE.

Types of Consequences

Consequences generally fall in to two categories, natural consequences and logical consequences. **Natural consequences** occur automatically in life. You do not have to do anything to impose a natural consequence. Examples of natural consequences include: toys being broken due to misuse, no clean clothes when laundry isn't put in the hamper, and not having time to play because your child dallied with his homework.

Knowing when to allow a natural consequence can be tricky. If your child has ADHD, some natural consequences may overwhelm him. A child with ADHD also has a hard time learning from natural consequences. He may need help cleaning his room, focusing on his homework, or caring for his belongings. On the other hand, protecting a child from facing the natural consequences of his actions does give him the wrong message. As an example of these issues, one author[67] suggests letting your child who neglected to put his socks in the hamper go without socks. Well, what if your child never has clean socks to wear? You may need to stand by and insist your child put his dirty clothes in the hamper. Expecting a child with ADHD to do the right thing on his own without help, may be unrealistic. The problem with natural consequences is that they have to suit your particular child.

Logical consequences are consequences imposed by parents, and that go along with a particular rule. For example, if your child repeatedly fails to put his things away, take his things from him. If two children will not share a toy, in spite of your intervention, take the toy away. If your child fails to come home on time, ground him. Remember, logical consequences should be simple, immediate and proportional.

Limit Setting With Teens

In some respects, limit setting with teens is easier than with younger children. There are more potential consequences for irresponsible behavior and you can make a written contract with your teen. The list of potential incentives for good behavior is also longer because teens want more privileges. It is very important that teens earn any increase in privilege they receive. Keeping a privilege should be contingent on good behavior. Rules and consequences prepare a teen for life in the real world..

Setting limits with teens can be more difficult because the drive for social dominance increases at puberty and teens want to be in control. Avoid dominance struggles with your teen by having clear rules and being consistent with consequences. If he perceives you are weak with regard to imposing consequences, your teen will constantly test you. During the times you impose consequences avoid talk of how your teen's bad behavior affects you. **Your teen's bad behavior is his problem, not yours.**

If you feel the need to talk to your teen about how his unruly behavior is affecting you and other family members, have this discussion at a time when you feel relaxed. Say to him something like "We all want to be close to you. You are part of our family, but your behavior is making you very hard to live with." Give your teen a chance to respond and try to have a discussion with him about how to get along better.

Steps to Impulse Control in Older Children and Teens

♥ Have your child identify his impulses (e.g. to be lazy, aggressive, bossy, angry, or sexual, to lie, steal or take risks). Your child should understand these impulses come from within himself and not from any triggers.

♥ Have your child acknowledge he has choices about how he responds to his impulses. It is good to try to control how we respond to our impulses.

♥ Encourage your child to avoid situations where he will be unable to control himself.

♥ Reward your child for avoiding temptation and controlling himself.

Getting Results From Limit Setting

Do not expect perfect results from limit setting. **At risk** children who have BOTH an increased drive for social dominance AND poor **impulse control** are very hard to live with. They constantly test and challenge their parents. They try to expose weakness so they can get their way. A parent's attitude is everything when it comes to dealing with these children. Do not expect your child to stop trying to push you! He will likely challenge you until he leaves the house and perhaps forever. Your limits are particularly important to this type of child. Limits and consequences should be stated in a normal, matter of fact tone. What good does it do for a parent to get upset all the time? His child is only doing what comes naturally.

The important point is that you seize every opportunity to correct your child. Be consistent. **Do not allow bad behavior to go unchecked because you are too tired to address it.** Inconsistent discipline is very bad for the **at risk** child because it does not foster the HABIT of **impulse control**. Everyone who cares for your child should know what undesirable behavior to set limits on. If your child is very impulsive, you have to be selective about leaving him with baby-sitters. An afternoon of incompetent supervision can erode away habits you have worked hard to establish.

If your child still needs a lot of correction, how do you know your limit setting is working? The purpose of setting limits is NOT to make your child compliant and submissive. **The purpose of setting limits is to teach your child what it means to live a good life.** If you have a good routine, a relatively organized home, and teach manners and safety you are doing all the right things with regard to building **impulse control**. Know that you are doing the right thing and feel good about yourself.

DO NOT EXPECT YOUR CHILD TO BE THANKFUL FOR ALL YOUR HARD WORK! If you expect thanks and appreciation, you set yourself up to be disappointed. **Your child is not capable of understanding the importance of what you are trying to do for him.**

Impulsivity In Emotional Expression

In order for empathy to develop, your child must be comfortable with emotion. Discomfort is the rule when emotions are overwhelming. **Model**, **teach** and **influence** applies to training your child to deal with anger and frustration. How can your child develop anger management skills if the adults in his life **model** the opposite? **Model** for your child restraint of your own anger and frustration.

Does Your Child Have a Hair-Trigger for Anger?

Your child has a hair-trigger for anger if:

1) He can't make it through the day without blowing up at least once.*
2) He blows up, loses control over his words and says things like "I hate you!"*
3) He blows up, then, throws things or breaks things.*
4) He doesn't necessarily blow up, but he stomps around and seems to be allowing anger to fester.*

*Children over the age of four should not do these things on a daily basis.

The **at risk** child is more likely to have 'a hair trigger' when it comes to anger and frustration. Studies show that impulsivity in the area of anger and frustration may be a temperamental risk factor for antisocial personality, ADHD[68] and addiction.[69] Impulsive children have a difficult time regulating all their many emotions, especially anger. If this describes your child, do not despair. Recognize that you will have to train your child to deal with his own emotions–especially anger and frustration.

You will also have to help your child slow down, relax and not become overwhelmed by other people's emotional displays. In addition to having a "hair trigger" for anger themselves, some **at risk** children become easily overwhelmed when they witness other people's emotions. Being overwhelmed by other people's emotions impairs the development of empathy[70] (see p. 61). The goal is not to make your child into someone he is not. The goal is to improve on his constitution to the point that his behavior is manageable and his anger does not rule him.

Showing restraint does NOT mean stuffing and never expressing any angry feelings. Showing restraint means expressing without losing control. Children generally learn about dealing with anger (and also sadness) when they see an adult cope without losing control. So, emotional expression is good, as long as it is not extreme. Also, if you are a single mom, make sure your male friends do not give your son the idea it is MACHO to be angry.

Teach your child anger management skills. A child needs to own <u>his</u> anger. He should understand that his anger comes from inside himself, not from you or his particular situation. He has choices about how he responds to people and situations. Angry displays are not a good way to communicate what he wants.

Anger management also involves sensing anger in its early stages. As a person starts to become angry, his muscles tense and his arousal level increases. Your child should learn to associate these sensations with the word anger. Lastly, he should develop an appreciation for the kinds of situations that make him angry. **Teach** him to avoid these situations, if possible. He can also stop interacting in any given situation when he feels he is starting to become angry. Some experts advocate teaching children to stop, take a deep breath and relax their muscles. (For more on this, see How to Raise a Child With a High EQ, by Lawrence E. Shapiro, Ph.D. and Hot Stuff to help kids Chill Out by Jerry Wilde, Ph.D.[71])

Tommy is six years old and has a hair trigger for anger. His adoptive mother and father are calm, gentle people and so do not really understand Tommy's anger. One day, Tommy was on the basketball court. Friends offered Tommy some soda pop his mother did not think he should have. When his mother stopped him from taking the soda, Tommy became extremely angry and started shouting "I hate you." He then took the basketball and started bouncing it very high and very hard, potentially endangering others around. When his mother tried to stop him, he ran away, as fast as he could, taking the ball to the other side of the gym so he could continue his angry behavior there. Tommy, eventually stopped bouncing the ball, but 15 minutes later, he still was not calm. He sat stewing under the bleachers, muttering to himself.

What should Tommy's mother do to help him? How could she have handled things differently? First of all, if Tommy is already a large child, helping him manage his anger may require more than one adult. He needs to be given a clear consistent message that losing control and blowing up is not acceptable. At the beginning of the episode, in the split second he started to become angry, his mother should have said, "You are becoming angry, stop yourself; you don't have to lose control. Let's talk about how you can feel better. Maybe, if you are thirsty, you can have some water or lemonade."

Some might say that bouncing the ball high and hard was a "good release" for Tommy. Remember however, that giving in to an impulse, and in this situation making an angry display, does not foster a habit of control. Tommy's mother should have taken the ball and had him sit for a time out, away from people. After the time out, she should have taken the opportunity to label the angry emotion, described the angry behavior and discussed alternative actions. "Instead of giving in to YOUR anger and blowing up, next time talk to me about how you feel. Tell me that you are thirsty. We can find you something else to drink."

Sometimes it is a good idea to ignore children who are pouting (like Tommy sitting under the bleachers). In this case, ignoring Tommy's pouting did him a disservice because ignoring did not help him manage his anger. His mother should have dealt with the pouting by saying, "You think you are getting even with me by pouting, really, you are only hurting yourself. You should learn to talk about what is bothering you. You will feel better if you give me a chance to help you."

Influence your child with the tone you set. Establish an atmosphere of peace in your home. Talk about the value of a peaceful home life. Be careful of the lyrics of the music you listen to and the content of the television shows you watch. If your child is excitable, loud television and music will not help him stay calm. Your anger-prone child should not watch cartoons in which the characters are predominately angry. Your home should be a soothing place.

Temper Tantrums

Temper tantrums are an example of impulsive emotional behavior. Temper tantrums are also a normal part of being a toddler. It is vitally important you not give in to temper tantrums. A parent who gives in to temper tantrums teaches his child a procedure for obtaining whatever he wants. No parent would intentionally **teach** a child to use nagging, hitting, whining, crying or tantrums to get his needs met. Accidental training occurs when these behaviors are rewarded.

I found that at times when my son threw a temper tantrum he had a legitimate gripe. For example, once he was hungry in the grocery store and so had a tantrum when I didn't let him open a box of food. Upon realizing I had made a mistake, I was left with a dilemma. How do I get out of this one? To make the best of the situation I said, "I see you're hungry, I'm sorry, I should have given you something to eat sooner." "I'll give you something, but not until you stop screaming and crying." This example illustrates giving the child incentive to control his behavior, sending him the message that you do not want the tantrum, and at the same time being **responsive** to his needs.

At the beginning of a tantrum, a parent may shudder to consider the possibility he may have to listen to screaming for an extended period of time (perhaps hours). I have also felt the embarrassment of my child throwing a tantrum in a public place. The crafty little ones know we do not want to listen to their screams and that we're embarrassed by the behavior. Their plan is to use this against us!

It is important for a parent to send a clear signal that he is prepared to win the battle of the wills. Any hesitation will be interpreted as a sign of weakness. Perceived weakness will lengthen the duration of the tantrum. Perceived weakness will also increase the frequency of future tantrums. In other words, as soon as he realizes a given tantrum will not get him his way, he will stop. (When he does stop, reward him for calming down and regaining control.) A child will start to grow out of tantrums once he realizes they are not effective at getting him what he wants.

Your at risk child may have difficulty with tantrums for much longer than other children. Keep working at it! What is your alternative? If you give up, things will get even worse. Realize that your child may not be able to maintain control because he lacks the brain structure to do so. You have to help him build that structure.

Food, Comfort and Impulse Control

Model and **teach** impulse control by not allowing a child of any age to grab for and gobble down his food. Consider making a habit of stopping before eating anything and being thankful. The goal is to **teach** the child to slow down and to insert time between wanting and gratifying. Just as physical stamina is conditioned, so too is **impulse control** acquired by conditioning. You cannot expect your child to run a marathon without daily workouts. **Impulse control** will get better the more it is exercised.

Compare the child whose desires are too quickly gratified with the child who has been conditioned to wait. Children who have not learned they can master their impulses are miserable. They are at the mercy of whatever impulse they are experiencing at any given moment. Parents who are overly gratifying think the gratification makes the child "happy." **On the contrary, happiness occurs when one realizes that one is O.K. even if impulses cannot be immediately gratified.**

In addition to waiting a little before eating, parents should set other limits around food. Don't allow your child to walk around the house eating and throwing crumbs everywhere. **Teach** him that restraint shows respect. Gently work with him to eat food that is more nutritious. Save the junk food he really likes for once in a while treats.

Children all display impulsivity with regard to their basic comfort. During maturation, they learn to tolerate discomfort.

It is important to teach your child to tolerate the discomforts of every day life. For example, do not allow your child to disrobe or remove his shoes in an inappropriate place just because he feels hot. Good parenting means more than just saying, "No, you can't take your shirt off here." Instead, acknowledge the feeling behind the impulse "Yes it's hot here. I feel like taking my clothes off too. What would you think if I took my clothes off? We put up with wearing clothes and shoes in this public place even when we don't feel like it."

Some of these suggestions may seem a bit nit-picky. My purpose is to show you that although setting limits with the at risk child is difficult, these children really need firm but gentle limits around nearly every aspect of their lives. The less internal **impulse control** a child has, the more he needs external limits. Limits should be set based on a child's ability not his chronological age. Do not give an impulsive child too much leeway, just because you feel he should be old enough to control himself.

The Drive for Affection

What about the drive to obtain physical and emotional closeness? Can a parent be too gratifying? For the **at risk** child the answer is NO. Remember that **at risk** children likely have less drive for closeness and so are less likely to act impulsively in this area. By analogy, think of a child who has just eaten his fill. He has less drive to eat and therefore will have an easier time waiting for more food. It is as if the at risk child becomes too easily satisfied by small amounts of closeness. That child needs to be encouraged to "eat" so he doesn't "starve" (emotionally speaking). Gratification of the need for love does not cause spoiling. **Spoiling happens when parents do not foster a habit of tolerance of discomfort and delayed gratification of the other basic drives.**

The Entertainment-Exploration Drive

In contrast to the drive to obtain human contact, **at risk** children are likely to have an increased drive to seek entertainment and therefore to explore. Furthermore, in **at risk** children the ability to be satisfied by a little entertainment is impaired. To use a food analogy, entertainment is to the **at risk** child as junk food is to the genetically obese child. The **at risk** child will try to consume more entertainment calories than is good for him. He will also behave more impulsively around obtaining gratification of his entertainment drive.

To describe what to do to entertain the **at risk** child, I must first establish what not to do. Do not allow your **at risk** child to be exposed to large amounts of high intensity entertainment. Keep him away from over stimulating media, computer games and group social situations. Just as cookies and cake are O.K. once in a while, high intensity entertainment is for once in a while, not every day. If you disregard this recommendation, your child will develop a high intensity entertainment habit. Once this habit is established, he will have even more difficulty finding joy in little things. He will continually complain of being bored by activities you think should interest him.

Find Joy in Little Things!

The ability to find joy in little things is a learned skill. Just like any other skill, finding joy takes practice. When you teach your child this skill and help him practice, you give him one of the keys to a happy life. You also immunize him against symptoms of ADHD and later addiction to substances.

If your child has already become "fat" from entertainment junk food, the only way to fix the problem is to put him on a "weight reduction" entertainment diet. The best way to help your child readjust and to enjoy the little things again, is to completely remove the high intensity entertainment for a while. If he is able to develop better habits, you can allow it again at a later date.

In the meantime, get him to expend his energy though physical activity, if possible, organized sports. Try to find small things that interest him. If he is young, have him play with puzzles, blocks, or LEGOS. Have him do art projects and enjoy music. An older child can also read books, build models or play a musical instrument. Try to help your school aged child develop meaningful hobbies. **The purpose of these hobbies is to teach him that interests that are worth pursuing take time and effort to develop.**

How do America's children spend their free time? Researchers from the University of Oregon surveyed 100 sixth graders and 100 8th graders to determine how these children spent their leisure time.[72] The most popular free time activities were listening to music, watching TV or videos, playing sports and playing computerized games. Reading was in the middle. Walking or running, cooking, writing and doing arts and crafts were not popular. Reading for pleasure declined with age and boys were more likely than girls were to report they spent NO time reading for pleasure.

Try to help your child establish a habit of reading for pleasure. He should spend at least thirty minutes a day most days reading. By reading books, magazines and newspapers, children build language skills. Having language skills can improve attention span and **impulse control**. If your child has a hard time focusing enough to read a long chapter book, have him read children's magazines. There are a number of excellent children's magazines. My favorites are *Click, Muse, Ranger Rick* and *National Geographic Kids*. These magazines will provide your child with entertainment, build his vocabulary, expand his horizons, and give him a chance to practice focusing. Ask your child to tell you about the articles he has read. You can use the articles to have meaningful conversations with your child.

I believe that learning to play a musical instrument is very important for **at risk** children. There is a great deal of scientific literature that links music education with both math and language achievement. Since many **at risk** children have problems learning math, they need all the help they can get. **Children who learn to play music have more advanced brain development than those who do not.**[73]

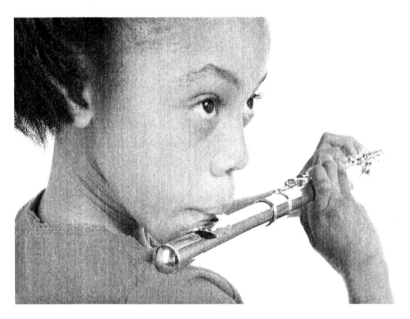

As I interviewed "experts" for this book, I found two schools of thought regarding music education. One group of "experts" subscribed to the theory that a child shows he is ready to learn to play a musical instrument when he willingly practices on his own. I strongly disagree with these experts. *As my daughter graduated from 8th grade, she won an award for playing cello. She started playing in second grade and she made rather slow progress. She NEVER willingly practiced on her own. (Interestingly, when I directed her to practice, she did enjoy playing.) As we left the graduation ceremony, she thanked me for forcing her to learn music and to practice her instrument. Maybe now she will practice on her own without reminders? I doubt it.* In the times we live in, the pull of the electronic media on children is so strong that most children have to be pushed to do anything other than sit in front of a CRT screen.

The second group of experts agrees with me that music education is so important to brain development that children should be required to learn music. The reason music education promotes brain development is that our brains are wired to perceive patterns. Exposing a child's brain to musical patterns and challenging him to reproduce them turns on (activates) many different areas of the brain. Since, defects in brain activation are related to ADHD, music education may combat the symptoms of ADHD. Music therapy is indeed becoming a popular adjunct treatment for ADHD.[74]

To investigate whether activation of the brain by music lessons is meaningful, researchers studied preschool children before and after piano keyboard lessons.[75] Children learning the piano were compared with children who received computer lessons, and children who received no lessons. The children who received piano lessons improved dramatically in their performance of a spatial-temporal reasoning test. Spatial-temporal reasoning is directly related to math ability. The benefit of music training lasts many years. Children with two or more years of instrument lessons perform significantly better on 8th grade standardized math tests.[76]

Many school systems offer voluntary music lessons. This music education is provided free of charge, or at very low cost. All you have to do is encourage your child to take advantage of the opportunities available to him. If you have the means, I suggest the following strategy. Have your child begin learning piano at 5 or 6 years of age. Tell him he will have to endure piano lessons and practice until second or third grade. At that time, most schools offer in school lessons and he can pick any instrument he wants. (My saying is, "You can learn any instrument you want, you just have to learn piano first.") By the time your child starts his in-school lessons, he will already know how to read music. Children have an easier time learning the basics of music on the piano. Have your child practice at least 15 minutes a day most days.

At risk children may be born with a different set point for the amount of stimulation they seek for themselves. **At risk** children seek a lot of outside stimulation. Another way to understand the harmful effects of too much high intensity entertainment is to consider that we all have the ability to adapt to different levels of stimulation. For example, a person accustomed to quiet is easily disturbed by noise. In the opposite extreme, during battle, soldiers adapt to very high stimulation levels. This causes them to feel empty when they return home. A child conditioned to too much high intensity video entertainment feels empty without the stimulation.

The set point for a desired stimulation level is not necessarily fixed and can be made more sensitive depending on exposure. If you can work to reduce the amount of stimulation your **at risk** child is exposed to, he will learn to be satisfied by smaller amounts of stimulation. **At risk children seek over stimulation even though they are harmed by it.** Therefore, parents must not allow **at risk** children to determine their own stimulation levels. Being **responsive** means knowing and doing what is best for your child even when he does not know or want to do what is best for himself.

Keep the amount of clutter that surrounds your child low. Starting at age 2, have him help you keep his living space neat. **Teach** him to be organized by providing places for him to put his stuff away. Do not give your **at risk** child an excessive number of toys. A messy over crowded room may be overly stimulating for him.

How often do we complain that our children are lazy? No wonder, high intensity media provide an easy out for gratification of their entertainment needs. It is easier to sustain attention to high intensity media. Overexposure prevents exercise of the "muscles" of attention span. Since developing attention span requires exercise of attention, children who sit in front of the TV passively watching become physically obese and mentally lazy.

Think about the link between attention span and the ability to enjoy little things. Playing music, doing art, reading books, and building models all require a child to work at concentrating. The more he exercises concentration, the better your child will get at it.

The better he is at concentrating, the more he will enjoy activities that require concentration. Remember also children naturally avoid developing parts of themselves that are difficult. If paying attention and using concentration are difficult for your child, you will have to work very hard to steer him in the right direction. Children who have learned to enjoy concentrating, and have meaningful hobbies develop **moral reasoning ability** more easily (p. 162). Teaching your child to concentrate is one of the most important things you can do for him.

YOUR CHILD'S LEISURE TIME

Your child has about 5 hours of free time Monday through Friday when he is not in school. He also has about 12 hours of "free time" on each weekend day. He should be required to do some chores everyday, and do his homework. If he plays a team sport, reads for 30 minutes and practices his musical instrument, he won't have much time to watch TV or play video games.

You may be asking "What about the new studies that show that children who play video games develop spatial reasoning ability?"

Some video games do require a child to exercise concentration and so playing these video games may be good for brain development. However, playing some of these video games also causes children to become physically agitated. Since, the child is seated while playing, there is no mechanism to release the physical energy that builds up. Furthermore, since video games are so stimulating they may be addicting and children who play them too much do not readily enjoy much else. You can help your child by limiting him to short periods of play (30 minutes) no more than 2 or 3 days a week. Have him exercise after playing video games and don't let him play right before bedtime as he may have difficulty falling asleep if he has become over stimulated.

If your child is physically active and enjoys sports or dancing, use this to his benefit. Participation in athletics can improve **impulse control** and attention. Martial arts can provide a similar outlet for both aggression and physical energy. Some children resist more quiet indoor activities. Without sports, these children have no activity in which to practice concentration.

Control over gratification of the entertainment drive is directly related to school behavior. Children who have a large need for stimulation are less likely to be able to adjust to the classroom experience. Remember, some **at risk** children feel empty without stimulation and this emptiness is very unpleasant for them. When these children seek to stimulate themselves and act out in school, they are only trying to relieve their own discomfort. **These children need help to better tolerate the discomfort and to reset the amount of stimulation they require.** If it is recommended your child take medication to improve his attention, also work with a doctor or therapist around helping him to develop better leisure habits. Perhaps if the medication can help him change his habits, he will need less of it as time goes on. The medication may serve to give him the boost he needs to exercise his "muscles" of attention and **impulse control**. Combined behavior therapy and medication may actually help strengthen parts of your child's brain.

Things that Help a Child with Attention and Concentration

- ♥ Adults that provide supervision and insist children finish projects they start.
- ♥ Learning to play a musical instrument.
- ♥ Reading for at least 30 minutes a day.
- ♥ Meaningful hobbies like sketching, painting and model building.
- ♥ Participation in organized sports or dance.
- ♥ At least 30 minutes of intense exercise a day.
- ♥ Good dietary and sleep habits.

Control over gratification of the entertainment drive is also directly related to work behavior in adults. "Pick a career you will enjoy" is an age-old adage. I would add, "Condition your child to be able to enjoy the career he picks." In order to be satisfied with life, a person must learn to be entertained by work.

There is a Buddhist saying, "Cook to cook." A person who cooks to cook, enjoys cooking as well as eating. When we fail to directly enjoy the work we do, and always look for some other reward in work, it is difficult to develop good work habits. Good work habits include punctuality, attention to detail, and persistence. It is extremely difficult for those who dislike work to be punctual, attentive to detail and persistent. Therefore, good work habits start with what I call a balance in pleasure (see p. 144). When we are entertained by and enjoy work, we develop balance in pleasure. Therefore, help your child learn to be entertained by work.

How to Positively Shape Your Child's Entertainment Drive

- ♥ Assign household chores and help your child learn to enjoy them.
- ♥ Let him pick some of the chores he does.
- ♥ Select chores that will teach him skills.
- ♥ Listen to music during chores.
- ♥ Do chores together rather than alone.
- ♥ Reward your child for doing a good job.
- ♥ Help your child pick meaningful hobbies.
- ♥ Enjoy hobbies with your child
- ♥ **Model** good work behavior.
- ♥ **Influence** your child with your positive attitude regarding work.

Things that Hamper a Good Work Ethic (by **negatively shaping the entertainment drive**)

- ■ Adults who **model** too much pleasure-seeking.
- ■ Over exposure to high intensity entertainment like TV.
- ■ Lack of a habit of physical exercise.
- ■ No meaningful hobbies.
- ■ Lack of goals for the future.

Born Without Fear– The Thrill-Seekers

Some children, many of them boys, are born without fear or with very little fear.[77] Usually this fearless behavior coexists with a great deal of physical energy. The parents of these children have a very difficult time keeping them safe. Remember that usually children use parents as a base from which to explore the environment without fear (Chapter 3). Well, fearless children do not feel much need for a "safe" parental base. Therefore, fearless children do not require as much parental support and reassurance. For this reason, fearless children are "at risk" to form weak relationships with parents. They simply do not need parents as much.

In addition to having high energy and fearlessness, **at risk** children also have a penchant for enjoying risk taking. Pleasure in risk taking can stomp out (extinguish) any natural fear an **at risk** child has. Psychologists tell us that fears go away when feared objects are associated with pleasurable thoughts or sensations. For example, a thrill-seeker afraid of heights might engage in sky diving. The thrill of the leap and the enjoyment of the view would extinguish the fear of heights.

In some children, the process of fear extinction happens naturally due to the child's enjoyment of dangerous activities. Since these children have a very large appetite for entertainment, they engage in thrill seeking activities more. When they enjoy dangerous activities, children become even more fearless.

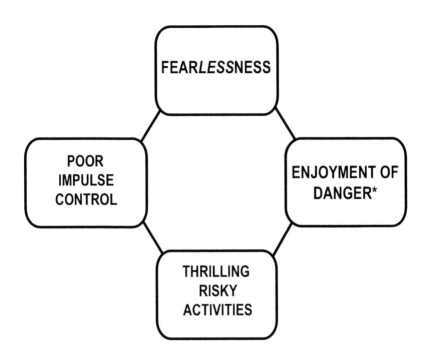

*Enjoyment of danger reinforces or strengthens fearlessness. You can overcome your fears by enjoying a feared situation.

While at a Lacrosse game rooting for my 12-year-old daughter, I became friendly with the mother of a teammate who had a little boy my son's age. He is an energetic 3 year old who keeps his mother on her toes. He enjoys jumping off high places. I observed as his mother held on to his hands as he repeatedly jumped off the 3-foot step of the grandstands. He was very persistent in demanding to jump without his mother's safety grasp. Which he did to his delight, all while his mother repeated the warning "You're going to get hurt!" Well, he did not get hurt and his mother's warning only served to teach him that mother is overly cautious.

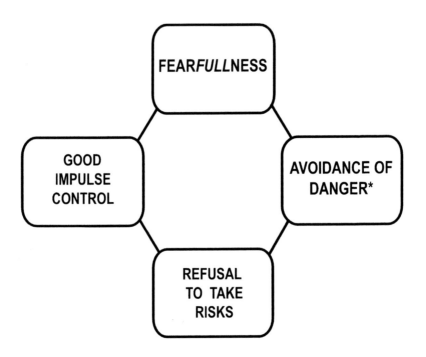

*Avoidance of danger reinforces or strengthens fear. If you are afraid of something and want to stop being afraid, the worst thing you can do is to run away from the feared object or situation. When you run away, you feel better. This feeling better strengthens the original fear.

The children in our place of worship play a similar jumping game. The fearless children jump off the 3-foot high stage gleefully. Other children look on– learning vicariously that there is nothing to fear. This shows that some children learn fearlessness both through their own experiences and by watching other children. The example I have used here, that of enjoying jumping off high places, is a normal behavior seen in many children. I am using this example to illustrate the manner in which adventuresome children lose their fears. Young children are not capable of realizing that they can jump 19 times, land on their feet without injury, then, on the 20th time break their leg. To them it is all good fun.

I am not suggesting we keep our children in a bubble, depriving them of their fun. However, we need to keep in mind that the at risk child may be a thrill seeker who will lose what little fear he was born with. Once the fear is lost, his risk taking will become more and more daring, and more and more rewarding. The more rewarding risk taking becomes, the more the child will prefer risk-taking activities to other activities. Remember that balance in pleasure is important for balance in life. If enjoying risky activities is more important to the child than enjoying relationships or other meaningful hobbies, there will be a problem. Because of risk taking, physical injury including head trauma is more common in at risk children and adults with antisocial personality disorder. Unfortunately, the brain damage that results from head trauma also worsens antisocial personality.

What then is the appropriate course for dealing with the at risk child's appetite for thrills? There is a long list of fairly risky activities children take up as hobbies, ATV riding, motorcycle racing, BMX biking, trampoline jumping, rock climbing, skiing, skate boarding…. the list goes on. I suggest the following 1) Any activity that the authorities have threatened to ban such as ATV riding (which has killed many children) be reserved for much older teens with a track record of responsibility. 2) If your child does take up a risky sport, take the opportunity to teach him about risk-taking behavior and the proper use of protective gear. The goal is to help him understand his appetite for risk taking and to get him in touch with any fears or concerns he may have. **He should develop a habit of moderating risk taking by assuming responsibility for his own safety.**

Using protective gear helps establish a habit of taking responsibility for personal safety. Teach your child that he may have "a blind spot" when it comes to seeing certain activities as dangerous. It is important that parents of fearless children oversee their activities. For example, do not just buy your child a skateboard and turn him loose to go sidewalk surfing without a helmet, pads or supervision.

Fearless children should be identified early as at high risk. Scientists have identified fearless children by their behavior in the first year of life! Fearlessness is likely one of the inherited traits that predisposes to antisocial personality and addiction. There is much scientific evidence that fearless children are physically different from other children.[78] They seem to have less inhibition in the brain compared to other children.

A strong relationship with mother or primary care giver is particularly important to the fearless child. Fearlessness also seems to impair the development of conscience (see pp. 170-174).

How to Manage Fears in a Child Who Is Relatively Fearless

Management of fears in children differs depending on the general level of fearfulness a child has (see p. 174). The strategy I outline here is for managing little fears in children who overall tend to be self reliant, outgoing and bold. Most children who are bold in comparison to other children still have some fears. Proper management of these few fears can really make a difference for the at risk child.

Parents of at risk children should capitalize on fear responses and use them to encourage closeness. When your child has a fear, stand by him and say, "I am here with you." Encourage him to turn to you if something scares him. Do not work too hard to discourage him from being fearful. **Especially avoid placing him in situations where he has to face and conquer his fears on his own.** For example, some people like to teach kids to swim by throwing them in deep water where they will either "sink or swim." A bold, athletic child would likely learn to conquer his fear of deep water and swim if placed in this situation. He would also receive training in being tough and ignoring his fears. This is not a good lesson for the at risk child.

*To my surprise, my self reliant, out-going, relatively fearless son suddenly developed fear of the dark at 30 months of age. He began to say, "I'm scared, dark" when encountering dark places. Each time I observed this I said, "I'm here with you, I won't leave you." "I will make sure the room is O.K." or, "I'll turn the light on." The alternative approach, to say, "Don't be a scaredycat, there is nothing to be afraid of." encourages children to toughen up. Instead, a relatively fearless, **at risk** child should practice listening to his fears and seek support when fear gets the better of him.*

STOP!

Fear is the emotion most tightly connected to the "STOP!" button. Fear influences the impulse control center more than any other emotion.

The forces that shaped the way humans respond to potential danger are complex. On the one hand, responding to danger with fear and avoidance (the STOP! response) is very important for an individual's survival. On the other hand, too much avoidance interferes with exploration. The fact that some humans are outgoing and have a strong drive to explore is very important to our species. This exploration is responsible for all human technical advances. Without fearless people, who would pilot the Space Shuttle? Who would go to the moon? Who would explore the ocean depths? Who would climb Mt. Everest?

Fearfulness, Conscience and Impulse Control

Why is understanding whether your child has a fearful or fearless temperament so important? The reason is that fearfulness predicts good conscience formation. The opposite is also true. Fearlessness makes conscience formation more difficult. Lack of a conscience is the main cause of antisocial personality disorder. Therefore, fearlessness is likely one of the most important inborn risk factors for this disorder.

The research connecting fearfulness and conscience formation is very interesting. In one study,[79] more than 100 young children were assessed as to level of fearfulness. These children were also tested for guilt in a laboratory situation where they were led to believe they had damaged valuable objects. Children who were most temperamentally fearful displayed the most guilt at 22, 33 and 45 months of age. Both the level of fearfulness and the level of guilt were stable personality characteristics of these very young children. Furthermore, children who had more guilt were least likely to violate rules at 56 months of age.

What mechanism connects guilt with fear? (For more on this see p. 171) I am going to offer a bit of speculation related to my observations of my own son. *One evening, when my son was 31 months old, he played with a motorized toy he really liked. It was time for dinner, and I told him he had to put the toy down and sit to eat. I gave him a chance to put the toy down on his own and go to the table. When he refused, I took the toy, picked him up and put him in his high chair for dinner. He threw an enormous tantrum and could not be consoled, even though I told him he could have the toy back after dinner. My usual strategy is to ignore these tantrums and allow them to burn themselves out.*

This time though, the crying and screaming was very loud and showed no signs of abating. His sisters complained that they could not enjoy the meal because of his behavior. I got up and moved the high chair, with the thought of just moving it far enough away to allow us to eat in some peace. Well, my son thought I was going to move him to the DREADED DARK PLACE! He said, "No mommy, no, I scared dark!" I said, "If you don't want me to move you away from the table, you will have to quiet, and eat your dinner." Miraculously, the tantrum stopped. Not only did the tantrum stop, but also he was so happy at not being banished to the dark place that he started to play and laugh with his sisters. He ate very well at dinner that night. He also completely forgot about the beloved motorized toy.

Fear of the dark provided my son with powerful motivation to control his angry emotion. In fact, I did not think he was even capable of the degree of control he showed that night. He rapidly shifted for extreme anger to joyfulness. His fear made him amenable to discipline. His fear made the threat of being separated from the rest of the family highly aversive. Without the fear, his motivation to control himself would have been much less. That night, at only 31 months of age, my son learned a very important lesson. He can shift from anger to joy if he tries. Fear leads to the development of **impulse control** as well as guilt.

Aggression and the Drive for Social Dominance

Your **at risk** child's greater drive for social dominance will extend into his relationship with you. It is this drive for social dominance that leads to oppositional behavior, as the child doesn't want to be told what to do. He wants to be in control. **Not only does he want to be Captain of his own ship, he wants you to be a deckhand!** This disrespectful behavior can be disheartening for a parent who has treated his child kindly and expects the love and respect to be returned. You can take some of this behavior in stride if you learn to view it as arising from a drive within your child.

What Is the Drive for Social Dominance?

■ Have you ever enjoyed being the center of attention?*

■ Do you enjoy it when other people look up to you?*

■ When you are with a group of people, do you like to be the one in charge?*

*If you answered yes to any of these questions, you have experienced the pleasure associated with gratification of your drive for social dominance. In animals, the dominance drive is important because social rank determines access to food, water and potential mates. In humans, things are much more complicated. The dominance drive is the force that makes us want to be first in line, to be on top, assume positions of leadership, and enjoy having control over others. It is also the force that makes us want to be admired and envied by others. The dominance drive makes us want to have the biggest house, fastest cars, nicest clothes and most attractive spouse, even if these things do not really bring us inner satisfaction. A person who is being ruled by his dominance drive seeks to be admired, envied and/or in control so much that he makes himself miserable. The misery happens because he can never be envied or admired enough or have enough control, to satisfy his drive.

Take power away from your child by **teaching** him about the drive to be dominant. In the role of **teacher,** you automatically assume a dominant position. You give your child the message that you have knowledge and experience he lacks. **Teach** your child that his problem with authority arises from yet another one of his drives being a bit excessive, or his impulse control center being weak. This information will help him not to take himself so seriously. Try to make light of the situation. "There you go again with that I want to be the boss stuff." "If you want to be the boss, you'll have to do my work, and I'll go out to play." Show your child that this behavior is absurd. You can directly label the dominance drive for older children.

The middle school years are a time when the dominance drive becomes more powerful due to the hormonal surges of sexual maturation.[80] The emergence of the drive for social dominance during puberty explains why the harmful effects of poor early attachment to mother and father (before age 5) may not be seen until adolescence (after age 12). It may seem as though a previously "perfect child" suddenly developed into a "terrible teen," when in reality, problems that began in preschool simply lay dormant until they were activated along with the drive for social dominance.

Oppositional Defiant Disorder (ODD)

ODD is the fancy diagnosis professionals give to a child with an out of control drive for social dominance. DSM IV defines ODD as "a pattern of negativistic, hostile, and defiant behavior lasting at least 6 months, during which four (or more) of the following are present:

1) Often loses temper
2) Often argues with adults
3) Often actively defies or refuses to comply with adults requests or rules
4) Often deliberately annoys people (p. 135)
5) Often blames others for his or her mistakes or misbehavior
6) Is often touchy or easily annoyed by others
7) Is often angry and resentful
8) Is often spiteful or vindictive

Emily has always been a beautiful girl. She has been daddy's little girl since the day she was born. Emily has also had the best of everything money could buy. She is now 14. Emily's mother loves her, but after Emily's birth, she suffered a severe depression that went untreated until Emily was four years old. Emily's mom was a stay-at -home mom, her dad was always very busy with his work. When Emily went off to kindergarten, her mom had a sinking feeling that due to her prior depression, she never really bonded with her daughter. Emily's mom worried about how her daughter would do in school. Emily did well in grade school however, and the problems of her preschool years were forgotten until this year. Emily now does what she wants, whenever she wants, and neither of her parents feel they can control her. It is apparent that Emily also does not want to control herself. The family goes to therapy together. During therapy sessions, Emily's parents express their love and concern for her, and their pain over her delinquent behavior. The expressed concerns fall on deaf ears as Emily is completely without remorse for the pain she has caused her parents. Emily's only concern is for her "friends" and her social position at school. She wants to achieve status with her peers and personal gratification by whatever means she can, even if it means hurting her parents.

In children like Emily, a poor relationship with parents does not become evident until the teen years. Some children may occupy themselves nicely in grade school achieving in school and playing sports, but then begin to fail in middle school. With puberty comes an increased drive for social dominance and sexuality. Suddenly these drives guide the child's behavior more than does his desire to achieve in school and pursue hobbies. The driven child becomes oppositional and this oppositional behavior taxes the already weak parent-child relationship.

Even if your middle school child is not excessively oppositional, expect him to have more trouble with his dominance drive, and therefore your authority. *When the girls were small, I greatly enjoyed the role of teacher. We spent hours together on science projects and homework assignments. Then, suddenly, when middle school came, both girls resisted my attempts to be teacher. They even questioned whether I had a knowledge base sufficient to help them. The real issue was that in the role of teacher, I was a superior, proving my competence to be in authority. If per chance I found an error in a girl's work…watch out! She became very defensive and did not want me to see her paper. I was baffled by this behavior until I realized its basis was a dominance struggle. I dealt with the struggle by acknowledging it, saying, "The day will come soon enough that you will know more than your mom. Until then be wise enough to take advantage of the help I can give you." This statement acknowledged the girls' desire to best me. They both seemed relieved to know I understood their feelings and was not put off.*

This silver-back male gorilla has an expression that tells everyone he is dominant!

Competent and Important

Your child has a true need to feel competent and important. This need comes partly from his drive for social dominance. If you fail to provide your child with opportunities to feel competent and important, he may become depressed or oppositional. Help your child feel competent and important by teaching him skills like home repair, gardening, cleaning and cooking. He can be your assistant as you do things. Begin this practice when your child is two years old. Do not shut your child out because you are in a hurry. Allow extra time for the chores to get done. How would you feel if you were often told "You aren't able to help, so just let ME do MY work"? If you give your child this message, don't be surprised when he is lazy and not helpful!

Just as over gratification of the entertainment drive is harmful, so is over gratification of the drive to be dominant. Social dominance is associated with higher levels of the hormones and brain chemicals that cause aggression. Therefore, allowing your child to dominate you will cause him to be even more aggressive and domineering. You must deal with him lovingly but firmly. You are the one in charge, not him.

Studies show that a secure loving parental relationship is more important for successful discipline of **at risk** children. I believe that one of the reasons for this is the dominance drive is moderated by love. Remember that affection counterbalances aggression and the dominance drive. The dominance drive is the cause of power struggles and resistance to parental correction. **A child in a loving mode can put his ever-present desire to be the one in charge aside for a while. Get your child to stay in a more loving mode by enjoying interests and activities with him. Show him tenderness and affection.** Ask him about the things he likes. Let him know you are interested in him and his point of view.

If you find you are becoming exhausted trying to provide discipline for your impulsive domineering child, please believe, you are not alone! There are many parents dealing with the same issues. All these parents know that worry for the well-being of a child is very draining. Feeling exhausted, drained and at the end of your rope is a sign that you and your child need professional help. The Chairman of the psychiatry department where I trained used to say in jest, "We need as many adults as we can get to gang up on the children." He wisely made the point that it sometimes takes more than one adult to rein in the dominance drive of an oppositional child.

How to Remain Captain of the Ship Even when the Crew Is Trying to Mutiny

- ♥ Encourage your child to stay in a loving mode.
- ♥ Enjoy interests and activities with him.
- ♥ Show him tenderness and affection.
- ♥ Have clear rules for behavior, enforce these rules consistently.
- ♥ Assume the role of teacher as often as you can.
- ♥ Avoid hypocrisy, model appropriate behavior.

About Cruelty and Violence

The impulses that arise from the drive for social dominance may also involve humiliation or abuse (physical and mental) of others. Retrospective interviews of those with antisocial personality disorder reveal that as children they were willful and controlling and many were also cruel toward pets and family members. However, not all those with antisocial personality and even not all psychopaths are violent. One scientist contends that our emotional response to cues of pain from others is inborn[81] (not learned). In other words, hearing or watching crying and screaming causes automatic discomfort.

This discomfort is a reflex in most people, even those with antisocial personality disorder.

There are psychopaths who, in addition to having severe guilt deficiency, also have no reflexive response to the screams of others. The expression of the drive for social dominance causes these psychopaths to become killers and rapists. If you have a child, boy or girl, who doesn't seem to be affected by observing pain in others, and is physically cruel toward animals, please seek help. **That child is at very high risk.**

The discovery that your child derives pleasure from cruelty may be shocking and repulsive to you. It is important that you deal with these impulses in the same way you deal with other impulses. **Teach** by identifying the impulse verbally. Have him acknowledge the feeling behind the impulse, and help him understand that we don't give in to those impulses. For example, if you observe your child being cruel to a sibling, stop him immediately. Say, "You seem to want to show him who the boss is" or "it looks like you are enjoying being mean." "What do you think about that?" Your child will probably reply that he doesn't know. That is O.K; just tell him that he has to stop himself from being mean.

A child should face consequences for being cruel that go beyond a verbal reprimand. Your first thought may be to "whack him" to exact retribution for the injured party and put him in his place. Remember that your job as a parent is to **model** appropriate behavior. Consider that hitting may not be productive since your child will learn by your example that hitting is O.K. if we can justify the reason. Instead, consider what he can do to make up for his transgression– perhaps pick up his sibling's toys or do some chore for you. If your child is so oppositional that he refuses to do what you ask, impose isolation in a place he will consider boring. Another strategy is to insist on keeping him with you constantly. "If I can't trust you to control your impulses, you will have to be where I can control you."

A Parent Says, "Sometimes it seems my child intentionally tries to provoke me!"

Children who have a strong social dominance drive, often argue, do and say things they know will upset their parents. In fact, it seems they do these things to get "a rise" from their parents. Unfortunately, parents often fall into the trap, becoming angry and giving an emotional display. Why would a child intentionally behave in a provocative manner? The reason is he enjoys observing his parent's emotional display and the feeling that comes with knowing he caused it. Evoking emotional displays in others is pleasurable because the act makes one feel powerful. Sadistic isn't it?

A parent who participates in these kinds of interactions with his child encourages sadistic behavior– pleasure at the expense of another's suffering. The child develops a habit of enjoying upsetting others. This is very bad. End the cycle by not reacting when your child tries to manipulate you. If you sense your child is trying to provoke you, say so. "It seems you are trying to provoke me. That is not a nice thing to do."

Dinner is over and Katie (age 11) knows she must clear her plate. She gets up from the table and plays with the dog while everyone else takes care of their dishes and heads for the kitchen. After petting the dog, Katie heads for the TV. Her father calls for her to bring her dishes. Katie ignores him and sits to watch TV. Upon being ignored, Katie's father becomes angry and starts yelling. Katie responds to the yelling, not by clearing her plate but by saying, "all you do is nag and yell." An argument ensues as Katie's dirty dishes sit, untouched, on the table.

Katie's father needs to do two things. First, he needs to stop being the best entertainment in town with his angry displays. Second, he needs to use the techniques of limit setting described in this Chapter to deal with Katie's behavior.

A Parent Says, "My child is a liar!"

Those with antisocial personality disorder begin habitually lying at an early age. Lying then becomes a craft they try to master and perfect. Lying in these individuals is related to a strong drive for social dominance. If a person can define reality for those around him by lying, he is like a god. Many antisocial individuals derive great pleasure from telling their tales. They sometimes do not even seem concerned about whether or not others believe them.

Habitual lying is a particularly worrying and troublesome behavior in **at risk** children. It is frustrating for parents, in part, because the parent being misled by lies is being treated like a subordinate. Children also tell tall tales to become the center of attention. Lying becomes a perverse form of entertainment for some children.

Habitual lying also occurs when parents are excessively critical. Children lie in order to avoid being yelled at, berated or spanked (more on yelling and spanking later). Children who lie under these circumstances may even believe in their own innocence. Impulsive children who are struggling to maintain a view of themselves as "good" sometimes lie, then, believe their own lies. In this case, the caregiver should instruct the child regarding the impulse that lead to the initial misdeed, and the impulse that led to telling the lie. "You lied because you didn't want to get in trouble for _____," "When you start to lie to avoid getting in trouble, you have to stop yourself." "If you're honest with me, you avoid making a second mistake, lying."

Many recent parenting books and magazine articles make light of lying behavior in children. The thought is that lying is a normal part of being a child. More often than not parents are advised just to ignore the lies. While this tolerance of lying may be the best approach for some children, I believe it is the wrong approach for the **at risk** child. If you notice that your **at risk** child habitually lies, you should be alarmed. The lying may be a sign of even deeper troubles. Parents should reward **at risk** children for telling the truth and use consequences to put a stop to habitual lying.

About Low Self-Esteem

Many behavior problems in children and adults are blamed on low self-esteem. Those with antisocial personality disorder are masters at using this excuse for their behavior. "The only reason I stole that $25,000 watch is because of my low self esteem. I just want to be as good as everybody else." The problem is that those with antisocial personality disorder do not have low self-esteem! They are grandiose and self-centered. In order to have low self-esteem, one must be capable of guilt. Since those with antisocial personality disorder have no guilt, they cannot have low self-esteem (see p. 171, for more on guilt).

Do not confuse low self-esteem with frustration of the desire to be dominant. The two are not the same. Children and adults with antisocial behavior patterns often become upset and frustrated when their dominance drive is thwarted. These feelings do not tend to last long as they soon move on to the next conquest. In contrast, low self-esteem occurs when a person realizes his failure to match his behavior with his own expectations. **Moral reasoning ability** beyond stage 0 is required for low self esteem (see the next Chapter). Do not excuse bad behavior by blaming its cause on low self-esteem.

It is important to address self-esteem issues in children that have intact **ability to love** and **moral reasoning ability** but have poor **impulse control**. Continued loss of control produces true low self-esteem in these children. Low self-esteem results *from*, not *in*, bad behavior. Low self-esteem is not a basic drive and it is only the basic drives and emotions that directly cause behavior.

There are many ways to help an impulsive child with his self-esteem. Helping him starts with labeling the child's problem and not defining the child by his problem. Statements such as "You are a good kid; you just struggle with your **impulse control.**" express empathy for an older child, while helping him to understand himself. Even very impulsive children also do good things. Make a habit of recognizing and praising the good things your child does.

Acquiring Possessions

As I finished the section of this book dealing with **impulse control**, I felt haunted by a feeling I had neglected to mention something very important. Then I thought, "What about stealing?" Is there evidence for a basic drive to acquire possessions? We call that greed! I inserted this section here because I am uncertain if the drive to acquire possessions is separate from the drive for social dominance, and the entertainment drive. Certainly, there are people who are content to be alone enjoying their many possessions. If social dominance were the only issue, possessions would only have value in the context of creating envy in or impressing other people.

We do know that stealing is common in **at risk** children.[82] Stealing has been called a "gateway crime" because children who begin stealing early (before age 12) are at very high risk to become antisocial personalities.[83] Children who steal do so for a number of reasons. Stolen objects have value to the child and the stealing is sometimes motivated by greed. "Thrill seeking" children with a strong entertainment drive steal for the thrill of stealing. Low brain arousal and low heart rate are common in **at risk** children. This low arousal is uncomfortable (boring). Activities, like stealing, that produce an "adrenalin rush" are particularly rewarding for children who suffer with abnormally low baseline arousal. Interestingly, medications that increase baseline arousal cut down on stealing behavior in **at risk** children. Children may also steal to impress their friends (another twist on the social dominance motive).

Elementary school aged children, caught stealing, should be considered for special intervention, especially if they are genetically at risk. Do not make excuses for a child's bad behavior. Many children who steal, steal from their own families and school, not from total strangers. Stealing is stealing, even if the victim is known to the child.

If you suspect that stealing is part of an overactive entertainment drive in your child (your child steals for the thrill of it), consider ways you can help him learn to redirect this drive. Physical exertion is the most natural and productive means to get the "adrenalin rush" the **at risk** child craves. Realize that if you have allowed your child to develop a high intensity media habit he may refuse to exercise. Helping your child may entail a complete restructuring of the way he spends his time.

Why Doesn't My Child Appreciate the Things He Has?

Parents must teach their children appreciation. Children who earn privileges and possessions appreciate them. A child who receives privileges and possessions independent of his behavior develops BOTH a sense of entitlement and a lack of appreciation. Raise your child to know he must work to earn the good things in life. If your child wants a privilege or possession, don't just give in. Use the things a child or teen wants to reward his good behavior.

The **model, teach, influence** approach applies to helping children learn to control their greed. Be careful not to **model** a lifestyle of greed. **Model** sharing and generosity instead. Let your child see you giving to charity and helping out your neighbors. **Teach** your child to share his belongings. Do not allow him to hoard toys, especially ones he never plays with. Help him box up unused toys and give them to charity. If your child badgers you incessantly to buy him things, take the opportunity to talk about greed. Tell him that it is not good for a person to place too high a value on having possessions. Do not **teach** him greed by shopping impulsively with him.

The danger of greed is that children may learn to enjoy acquiring and possessing things as opposed to enjoying and loving people. You do not want your child to view you as merely a supply source for the possessions he wants.

When my daughters were small, I became distressed at the fact that holidays and birthdays centered on "getting stuff." I wanted them to enjoy holidays as such and not just look forward to presents. They were only four and six years old when I sat them down and said "look, we can either buy you the things you need year round as you truly need them, or, you can get presents on your birthday and the holidays." Surprise! they both chose to get stuff as needed year round! Not that they didn't get little treats for their birthdays and the holidays, but we got away from what I felt was a misplaced focus. Birthdays and holidays are relatively stress free for me now because I don't worry about buying them things. As a family, we enjoy the holidays together, celebrating family, not the stuff we got.

Sex

As your child nears adolescence, his sex drive will become increasingly powerful. At risk children with poor **impulse control** are likely to have trouble controlling their sexual impulses. Try to shield your child from early exposure to sexuality. The older he is when he first experiences his sexual impulses, the better off he will be. An older child will have had more experience controlling his other impulses. The more he is exposed to material of a sexual nature, the more your child's sex drive will be activated.

Model, teach, influence also applies to the area of sexuality. Make sure the adults in your child's life **model** responsible sexuality in their dress, talk and behavior. **Teach** your child about sexual impulses when appropriate. Discuss the idea that these impulses cannot be acted on irresponsibly. A teenaged boy or girl who becomes sexually promiscuous is likely practicing a lifestyle of using other people as objects of gratification rather than appreciating them as companions. Discuss the importance of companionship and friendship with your teen. Help your child learn to be sexuality responsible when he is mature enough to handle it. **We don't want to be controlled by the impulses that arise from our drives.**

Influence your child with the tone you set and the atmosphere of your home. Do not keep pornographic (sexually arousing) material in the house; this includes certain well-known clothing catalogues. Remember *Playboy* magazine, *Victoria Secret*, and some music videos are really pornography but are now considered socially acceptable. Sexually explicit talk is also considered O.K. I am not suggesting that talk of sexuality be forbidden. I am suggesting that talking about sex is sexually arousing, and we need to encourage our teens to have control over how they respond to the impulses that come from their sex drives. Things that are accepted by the popular culture may cause harm to your child by encouraging him to act on his impulses.

Talk to your daughter about owning the sexual impulses that are leading her to dress provocatively. Don't just tell her to change her clothes. Some girls may be unaware that it is their own sex drive that makes them want to dress a certain way. They also need to know what the males that see them are thinking!

Once, my daughter was upset because I didn't want to take her scantily clad friend on a trip to a public place. I nicely asked her friend (who was only 14) to put a shirt on over herself. I was pretty sure her own mother hadn't seen her before she left. On that same trip, there was a sad, scruffy looking, homeless man standing on the street corner. The girls gasped when they saw him. After expressing sympathy for his condition, I said, "Just think girls, for every cute guy that sees you in your short shorts, and halter top, there's a guy like that who sees you!" They were appropriately "grossed out" and the point was made.

Summary of the Basic Drives

Along with emotions, the basic drives motivate all human behavior. Some of the basic drives are intertwined. For example, in adults, the sex drive is intertwined with the drive to obtain closeness. Sexuality can also be used to achieve social dominance. **One of the keys to a satisfying life is moderation, balance and control over the basic drives.** How we define the stimuli that entertain us is vitally important. If we work on a habit of enjoying little things and closeness with others, peace and satisfaction will come more easily.

DRIVE TO:	DEFINITION	CONSEQUENCE
Obtain Food and Comfort	Ensures sufficient food and water intake.	Learning to wait can help reduce impulsivity. Over gratification leads to laziness and obesity.
Obtain Closeness	The drive for physical and emotional intimacy.	The child needs to have intimacy freely available to him. The child needs to enjoy intimacy.
Explore and be Entertained	The drive to have fun, thrills and excitement. The drive to explore. This drive is related to fearlessness.	Over indulgence leads to chronic boredom. Fearlessness leads to injury and impairs conscience development. Exploration is important for human survival.
Social Dominance	The drive to be in control.	Social dominance is responsible for leadership, aggression and cruelty.
Acquire Possessions	The drive to have belongings.	Impulsive greed leads to stealing. Greed is related to lack of balance in pleasure.
Have Sex	The desire for sex.	Impulsivity leads to pregnancy, venereal disease and trauma.
Procreate	The drive to have children.	Teen pregnancy.

Balance in Pleasure

There are two ways not to be ruled by drives.

- ♥ The first is to have a well-developed "STOP!" button.
- ♥ The second is to achieve "balance in pleasure." The pleasure balance is not the same for everyone, but a good balance involves:

1) Tolerance of discomfort*
2) Moderation in trying to get pleasure**
3) Well-placed priorities***
4) The ability to be easily entertained****

*Unfortunately, discomfort is part of life.

**Whenever drives are excessively gratified, there is harm.

***Well-placed priorities allow a person to decide, thoughtfully, which drives to act on.

****The ability to be easily entertained allows a person to distract himself and direct himself away from over gratification of the other drives. **Lack of balance in pleasure makes a person vulnerable to addiction (see Chapter 7).**

Helping your child achieve **impulse control** involves both helping him to develop his "STOP!" button and helping him to achieve balance in pleasure. Your child's "Stop!" button will be influenced by many small factors which together may add up. Diet, allergies, and the amount of sleep and exercise your child gets may all influence his "Stop!" button performance.

Seek a recommendation from your health care provider for nutritional supplements for your **at risk** child. Although this has not been scientifically proven, some parents believe that identifying food allergies does seem to make a difference in **impulse control**. In ALL children and adults, sleep deprivation worsens **impulse control**. Make sure your at risk child gets enough exercise. Perhaps medication could be avoided in some children **IF** problems with **impulse control** were addressed with diet, exercise, sleep, and parental training. If you institute a program of diet, exercise, sleep habits, rewards, limit setting and leisure time activities, you know you are doing all YOU can for your child. If your child still requires medication, do not feel guilty, work closely with his doctor. Medication is necessary for some children.

Organization and Time Management

If your child is an adventurous risk-taker with a strong entertainment drive, organization and time management will be a special challenge for him. He may complain that using time management skills and taking time to stay organized are "boring." Well, of coarse these things are boring compared to the many adventures your child seeks! **Teach** him that he must learn to put aside his need for excitement in order to have overall well-being. The key to organization is to limit the amount of "stuff" you and your child have to deal with. **At risk** children really like having *new* things because they find the unfamiliar exciting. The problem is that new things quickly become old things, build up and create clutter.

Your child may try to impulsively add new activities to his schedule. Remember any *new* sport or activity will be exciting at first. Resist the temptation to over schedule your child. It is more important for him to learn to stick with activities and to master skills than to try many new things. Leave enough time at the end of each day for your child to organize his school work, toys and belongings.

He Can't... or He Won't?

Is it that your child can't do the right thing or is it that he won't do the right thing? The truth is that sometimes your child can't make himself want to do important things. In **at risk** children and adults, the reward systems (that make us want to do things) do not function properly. For example, have you ever noticed that your child is able to clean his room when he wants to, but when you send him in to clean, he sits on the bed appearing dazed? Or, perhaps your child repeatedly forgets to bring home his homework but always remembers he has baseball practice.

This problem with the experience of reward is at the heart of addiction. One insightful addict once said to me, "I want to quit smoking but I can't, and I should stop drinking but I don't want to." Start early **teaching** your child that we have to train ourselves to experience little rewards in life and we have to set our routines so that we have incentives to get things done. Will power is good but of limited practical usefulness. The role of reward in our lives is much more powerful. **We CAN learn to take control of rewards!**

Can you eat your vegetables even when the taste is disgusting to you? How hungry do you have to be before you can force yourself to eat a food you find unpleasant? All of the basic drives described in this Chapter operate the same way. There is a set point for reward based on need. A large need due to increased drive (either from brain chemistry, hormones, deprivation or habit) leads to a larger reward. For some people, the experience of deprivation, reward and satiety is not as well regulated as it is for others.

Armed with this understanding of drives and reward, think again about punishment. Say your child didn't clean his room because he couldn't make himself want to. Will yelling at him fix this problem? Yelling only works if your child cares whether or not YOU are upset. If your yelling makes him anxious, his ability to force himself may be further reduced. If you want your child to clean his room, you have to help him want to do it by rewarding his efforts and keeping him company for part of the job.

If there is a job to be done, break it down into smaller tasks that take 10 minutes or less to complete. When each task is done, reward your child. Let him learn to take pride in each little job well done.

Realize that your child will always be to some degree mastered by his drives. Learning to live with our drives is like surfing. Every once in a while you catch a big wave and really have fun. The bigger waves bring more fun with a greater risk of drowning! Most of the time, we have to learn to be satisfied safely hanging ten on the smaller waves. We can't control the waves mother nature sends our way but we can choose which ones to ride.

Mood Disorders

Poor **impulse control** may also caused by a mood disorder. The most common example is an irritable mood related to depression which gives rise to temper outbursts. Mood disorders also disturb balance in pleasure. An abnormally elated or manic mood can be associated with impulsive pleasure seeking or risk taking. In children showing extremes of behavior, it can be very difficult to sort out the presence of a mood disorder verses other problems. Mood disorders are common in the biologic relatives of individuals with antisocial personality, addiction, and ADHD. Mood disorders may be misdiagnosed as ADHD in children.[84] Caretakers should be aware that the **at risk** child might also be at risk for depression and bipolar disorder (manic depression).

There is a rule (well-known to mental health professionals) that says when a mood disorder is present, it is very difficult to discern any of the underlying problems with **ability to love** and **impulse control** that produce character disorders. Mood disorders can mimic disorders of character and character disorders can mimic mood disorders. For example, a depressed child can be more impulsive and can lack the ability to enjoy loving relationships.

It pays to recognize when a child may have a mood disorder. Mood disorders are more easily treated than are problems with **impulse control** and **ability to love.** If you suspect your child is depressed or manic, please seek competent professional help. Appropriate treatment will prevent the toxic effects of the mood disorder on your child's development. A depressed child will have trouble concentrating in school and maintaining friendships. He will, therefore, fall progressively more behind in his intellectual and emotional development the longer the disorder goes untreated. Depressed children are also chronically disinterested in activities. Thus, they can "look like" those children who have had over gratification of the entertainment drive.

News commentators have pointed out that many of the teens that have used guns to commit murder in the past few years were taking antidepressant medication. It may be that antidepressants predispose to violence in some children and adults. However, also consider that a physician prescribing antidepressants has to try to figure out if the cause of a particular set of behaviors is related to depression or to developing antisocial personality. Can you see why a physician would want to give a young person the benefit of the doubt? Thus, it is likely that some children are wrongly prescribed antidepressants and, unfortunately, it is also these children who have a propensity toward violence.

If you are considering whether to agree to antidepressant treatment for your child, do not base your decision on news reports. Consider with your physician, the risks and benefits likely for your individual child. Keep in mind that the very toxic effects untreated depression can have on development may be worse than the real risk of medication side effects. Also, ask your physician to be frank with you regarding potential character problems he sees in your child.

Physicians are like everyone else, they don't necessarily want to insult their clients with an uncomplimentary diagnosis. Would you rather hear "Your child is depressed" or "Your child has conduct disorder, the precursor to antisocial personality"? I rest my case. Please, ask your physician directly how sure he is of the mood disorder diagnosis.

Our family has survived the moody preteen years of two girls. When I observed the typical irritable or tearful outbursts, I took the time to explain to the girls what mood is. **A mood, irritable, sad, elated or neutral is a physical state.** This physical state is influenced by season of the year, hormones (both stress and sex hormones), sleep pattern, diet and exercise. Therefore, our lives will come under the influence of many different moods. Some of these moods may be totally unrelated to the goings on in our lives because they are of a physical nature.

The important thing is to try as hard as we can, not to be ruled by our moods. Certainly, an irritable mood does not give one carte blanche to lash out abusively at family members. We have to take responsibility to treat each other with love even when we feel irritable. For people who may develop repeated episodes of mood disorder, learning to function through a mood is part of the treatment of the mood disorder. (Medication may not be perfect at keeping a person's moods stable.) If in an episode of depression one lashes out abusively at loved ones, one only alienates one's self further. Lashing out also leads to more guilt. In trying to act lovingly in spite of feeling sad, many can find some relief from sadness.

CHAPTER 5

MORAL REASONING ABILITY

Moral Reasoning Ability Is Unique to Humans

The **ability to love** and exert **impulse control** are qualities other intelligent mammals possess. I know my dogs love me. I have also been able to train them not to steal food from my little son, even when he waves his bites of meat around. **Moral Reasoning Ability** is unique to humans. **Moral Reasoning Ability** is the process by which we conform our behavior to a set of values. By believing in a set of values and conforming our behavior to our beliefs we become "good" people. The process by which children acquire a value belief system and learn to conform their behavior to that system is called moral development. I have provided a brief summary of moral development and addressed issues unique to the **at risk** child.

Guiding Your Child through the Phases of Moral Development

The ability to understand morality grows in stages along with a child's ability to reason. Social experiences also influence moral development. Children are generally in Stage 0 through age 2 or 3 until the rudiments of conscience are formed. Once a child begins to develop a conscience, he moves into stage 1 and stage 2 and is less self-centered.

The Phases of Development of Moral Reasoning[85]

Phase (Stage) (Usual Age)	Description	Primary Belief
Preconventional Phase (Stage 0) (0-2)	No Moral Development	I Should Always Get What I Want
Preconventional Phase (Stage 1) (2-6)	Punishment Orientation	I Should Avoid Being Punished
Preconventional Phase (Stage 2) (2-6)	Pleasure Seeking Orientation	I Should Do What Will Get Me Rewarded
Conventional Phase (Stage 3) (6-adult)	Good Boy/ Good Girl	I Should Be Nice
Conventional Phase (Stage 4) (6-adult)	Authority Orientation	I Should Follow Rules And Respect Authority
Post- Conventional Phase (Stages 5 &6) (14-adult)	Social Contracts And Moral Values	I Should Do The Right Thing

When parenting preconventional (preschool aged) children, the goal is to help them see that their behavior is connected with good and bad consequences for themselves. Through the use of rewards and consequences as described in Chapter 4, parents empower children to seek positive reward and to avoid punishment. At the same time preschool aged children are learning the concepts of reward and punishment, they are also developing an appreciation for the human dominance hierarchy (authority). In addition, children of this age are also beginning to develop empathy. The combination of appreciation for reward/punishment, understanding of authority, and rudimentary empathy enables children to develop a conventional understanding of morality.

Children who have an understanding of morality typical of the Conventional Phase want to be "nice," gain social approval, and respect authority. It should be noted that many grade school children go back and forth between the preconventional and conventional views of morality. Furthermore, the concept of reward for socially acceptable behavior and consequences for misbehavior has to be reinforced by parents through the teen years.

It is one thing for children to want to be good and respect authority (Stages 3 and 4). Knowing the principles behind rules (having values, stages 5 and 6) allows a child to extend good behavior into new unsupervised situations. To know and understand the principles behind rules requires advanced moral reasoning ability. During the time your child is in your care (ages 0-18) he learns to categorize the rules you have given into a moral code of values. For example, the rules about personal hygiene become the value "take care of your body and appearance." The rules for manners become "treat another person the way you would want to be treated." This is why imposing rules and giving reasons for rules is so important. Giving reasons for rules enables a child to develop values. Rules that you set at home form the basis of the value system your child will carry with him for life.

How to Prevent Disordered Moral Development

Although they can recite the rules for behavior, those with antisocial personality disorder, especially psychopaths, do not possess a moral code they ***believe in***. Many addicts have lost their belief in the values they once held dear. Children with untreated ADHD may have a difficult time developing moral reasoning.

Take a look at the stages of development of **moral reasoning ability**; you will notice that those with antisocial personality disorder remain fixed at stage 0! They never get beyond "I should always get what I want." They do not even get to the first half of the Preconventional Phase. Although they are at times motivated to "get reward" the avoiding punishment part is beyond them.[86] In terms of **moral reasoning ability,** an adult with antisocial personality disorder has the intelligence of a three year old– at best!

Why do those with antisocial personality remain fixed at stage 0? In my opinion, there are three main reasons those with antisocial personality disorder fail to develop a conscience and remain fixed at stage 0. First**,** impaired moral development in antisocial personality is related to impaired **impulse control**. Second, an out of control drive for social dominance prevents moral development in **at risk** children. Third, impaired moral reasoning is related to an impaired ability to respond to punishment (negative consequences).

Moral reasoning ability starts when parents train impulse control. When parents establish clear rules for behavior in the home, and require a child to exercise restraint over his drives and emotions, they set the stage for **moral reasoning ability** to develop. Without **impulse control**, rules and consequences, there can be no moral reasoning. Since those with antisocial personality disorder have impaired **impulse control**, moral development freezes unless there is an ***unusually*** good relationship with parents (more on this later).

Using moral reasoning in our daily lives is a two-step process. The first step requires understanding a set of beliefs about what is important. The second step is doing what that set of beliefs tells us to do. This is why poor **impulse control** can impede the development of **moral reasoning ability**. A child who frequently breaks rules due to impulsivity has two choices when it comes to *believing in* a value. His first choice is to view himself as "bad" because he cannot abide by rules. The second choice is to view rules as "stupid." A child who views rules as "stupid" cannot develop values. **It is important for the caretakers of an impulsive, at risk child to help him see that he can be "good" if he acknowledges he at least believes in the rules and makes a good faith attempt to control himself.**

Those with antisocial personality disorder and those with addiction also have a hard time connecting future consequences with present actions. It is as if they cannot predict the future the way the rest of us can. Learning to avoid negative consequences is central to the development of moral reasoning. You should start early VERBALLY **teaching** consequences to your **at risk** child. Do not just pull your toddler away from danger. Explain the danger and do not let your child continue on without verbally repeating your warning. For example, I taught my son early that hot things could burn. The thought to do this started when I observed he tried to eat rice that was a little too hot. When I saw him wince, I said, "Burn you!" He was only about 14 months old. He repeated, "Burn you," and, seemed to understand. As time went on he was able to say, "Burn you!" in response to the stove, fireplace and candles. He then learned to respond, "Hurt you!" to knives and cars on the street, and "boom-boom" to high places.

Remember, *words are powerful, use your words*. Do you see the difference between starting early with VERBAL MESSAGES and raising a child in a relatively non-verbal environment? Most parents would not allow a child to handle fire, play with knives, run in traffic, or teeter at the top of high places. However, just stopping and/or punishing an activity does not adequately teach consequences. **At risk** children need verbal messages about consequences repeated over and over. Parents should encourage verbalization of consequences BY **at risk** children as soon as they are old enough to talk.

When you see your child about to act on an impulse, stop him, then explain what you see as the potential consequences of his acting on the impulse. Do not forget to identify the impulse for him. If time permits, verify his understanding by getting him to repeat your teaching. For example, your child is playing ball in the yard. The ball starts to roll into the street. Stop your child and say, "you are tempted to run into the street without looking, stop yourself!" "If you don't stop and look, you could be run over by a car." Another example involves manners. Say your child is at a party and he is hungry. He is first in line to get the cookies. You see him pick up the entire plate to keep all the cookies for himself. Stop your child and say, "You are hungry and want some cookies. You cannot take them all. Other children here are hungry too, they also want cookies. We have to share."

By verbally teaching your child, you establish your parental authority in a loving way. This method is far more effective for **at risk** children than is yelling at them or spanking them if they do something wrong (p. 200). If you and your child happen to see other children acting in an unsafe way, use the opportunity to talk to your child. "Kristen's riding her bike without her helmet on. If she falls, she'll be like Humpty Dumpty… All the King's horses and all the King's men won't be able to put Kristen back together again!" Not every teaching needs to be done sternly and seriously. Keep your child's attention by using rhymes and humor when you can.

Games that require the child to plan ahead and predict what will happen next encourage the development of the part of the brain involved with consequences. Most of the common board games fall into this category. The most sophisticated are Chess and Risk. Checkers and Monopoly are also good, as are some strategic card games. Take time out on rainy days to play these kinds of games with your grade school child. Observe how he plays the games; **teach** him about strategy and consequences.

Temptation: A Useful Concept

Temptation happens when something entices us to do the

wrong thing. Children and adults with poor impulse control have to make a special effort to avoid temptation. If a person lacks will power or impulse control, he is more likely to do the wrong thing if faced with temptation. Such a person can do the right thing more often if he avoids temptation. Protect your child from doing the wrong thing by keeping him from temptation. Teach him that it is important to avoid temptation and give him progressively more responsibility for his own avoidance. For example, if your child has a weight problem, do not keep junk food around. Help him make the right choices regarding food. Then, when he goes out to eat with the family of a friend, encourage him to make good choices even when you are not there. Similarly, if your teen lacks the maturity to handle being around members of the opposite sex without engaging in inappropriate behavior, then don't allow him unsupervised time. Only allow him to be on his own when he shows he can cope with temptation on his own.

Since avoiding punishment will remain a special challenge for some **at risk** children, parents should not rely on parenting techniques based on yelling or physical punishment. Parents who rely excessively on yelling and physical punishment to control behavior fail with **at risk** children. Consequences for misbehavior as described in Chapter 4 work better for **at risk** children than does yelling and spanking. The reason is that these children become easily overwhelmed. When overwhelmed and overloaded, **at risk** children turn off and cannot learn. **Instead of relying on punishing bad behavior, the parents of at risk children have to verbally teach their children and make a special effort to keep them away from temptation. Keep your child away from situations where his ability to control his impulses will be over taxed.** Talk to your child. Help your child understand himself. It is O.K. for him to realize that his ability to control his impulses is less than that of many children.

Successfully conquering temptation builds and strengthens **impulse control** and morality. In a classic experiment, researchers showed children an interesting battery-operated robot.[87a] The researcher then told the children not to play with the toy without supervision. To deter playing with the toy, the researcher used a strong warning with half of the children and a mild warning with the other half. Children in both the strong and mild warning groups controlled their impulses to play with the toy. The children returned several weeks later and met a different researcher who left them alone in a room with the robot without giving any instructions. About 80 per cent of children given the strong warning now played with the toy. Interestingly, the majority of children given the mild warning, did not play with the robot. How can we explain these findings? When a child makes a conscious decision to exert impulse control of his own free will, that decision is likely to guide his later behavior. If a child is coerced and so does not make his own decision, he is unlikely to learn a moral lesson.

The Importance of the Bond with Parent

During moral development stage 1, children first begin to evidence conscience and values. Some **at risk** children can only move to stage 1 (that of obedience) due to an exceptionally strong relationship with their parents. Other studies have examined the willingness of young children to do what mother and father ask.[87b] These studies reveal a direct effect of the quality of the parent-child relationship on obedience. **More punitive parenting styles are indeed associated with LESS obedience in some children.** This is partly because excessive punishment damages the parent-child relationship and makes a child reject his parent's teaching. You want your **at risk** child to think of you as his teacher and mentor. In fact, since the application of physical punishment drives a wedge between parent and child, excessive punishment (which destroys the parent-child relationship) is very bad. In a misguided attempt to instill **impulse control** and **moral reasoning ability** through punishment, parents can damage **ability to love**. **Ability to love** is required for conscience.

For **moral reasoning ability** to develop beyond stage 0, the parent must keep himself in the center of the **at risk** child's world for an extended period of time. If the parent is the center of his child's world, the child looks to the parent for teaching, comfort and pleasure. The parent can therefore use himself as a reward for good behavior. A parent should not allow a child to have more than minimal independence until he moves into the obedience stage (stage 1); this may not happen until late grade school in some children. Prior to stage 1 children should be kept physically close and should be well supervised.

For the **at risk** child, the motivation to be good is not necessarily to avoid punishment. The motivation to be good is to obtain the rewards of closeness with his parent. If the child does not love and enjoy his parent, there is no reward for closeness. Remember that time spent together, shared activities and **responsiveness** are the keys to an enjoyable loving relationship. Therefore, if a child is on shaky ground regarding obedience, giving him too much time alone to entertain himself or too much time to have his intimacy needs gratified by peers, will harm an already weak relationship. You do not want your young child to get the idea he is fine without you. If your child is oppositional, he needs more **responsiveness**, teaching, shared activities and time. (I told you this was going to take more work than you bargained for.)

An over active drive for social dominance may also impair the **at risk** child's ability to abide by rules, and learn morality. He may understand that there are rules, but since he is the Captain of the ship, it is his prerogative to change them according to his desire. If an **at risk** child is allowed to dominate his parent, chaos will ensue. The child needs an understanding of parental authority in order to learn to abide by rules and develop **moral reasoning ability** Unfortunately, too many parents choose to assert authority through physical and verbal aggression rather than through the teaching of consequences. When exposed to this aggression, **at risk** children become aggressive.

Your Child, *Your* Helper

Giving an allowance is a good way to assert authority. You are the one holding the money and will decide whether he has performed well enough to deserve it. Before you hand over the cash, give your child an evaluation of his helpfulness. Attach reward to his performance of work under your authority. If you are a single mom, be careful not to give your son the idea he is "man of the house." As "man of the house" he may feel he is dominant over you and resist your authority.

Start early encouraging your child to be your helper. Keep him with you as you do your chores. Assign him tasks to do with you. 2-3 year olds can pick up toys, help carry in the groceries, put items in the trash, help with laundry, help with pets, help water the yard and help wash the car. They can also bring you things and turn the TV on and off. Sometimes as children get older, their eagerness to be helper decreases. Do not let your child off the hook with chores because you feel he deserves to play.

When a child is taught to believe he deserves to play while others are working, HE DEVELOPS A SENSE OF ENTITLEMENT. A child with a sense of entitlement does not respond well to correction. Let him play, but only after he has done his chores.

Assert YOUR authority by making the household rules clear early on. Use verbal teaching, rewards, and limit setting to establish yourself as Captain and run a tight ship. Have your child do chores; don't wait on him too much. If you wait on him, he will only view you as his servant. Place your child in the position of being YOUR helper.

Respect

Respect is important because it is an acknowledgement of the order of the dominance hierarchy. We treat our elders and those in authority with respect because of their higher status. Those in authority treat underlings with respect because it is the duty of higher ups to care for underlings. This mutuality makes the social world go around. Insist your child speak to his elders with respect and restraint.

Many young children understand the concept of a social dominance hierarchy. It is hard to watch a television show about social mammals without hearing a discussion of the concept of social dominance. I recently got a chuckle hearing a group of first graders at the zoo talking about the Alpha wolf and others talking about the Silverback male gorilla! **Teach** your child the importance of abiding by the hierarchy humans have set up. Ask him what happens when a subordinate wolf challenges the Alpha or a subordinate gorilla challenges the Silverback. You may be surprised at how much understanding your child has.

Teach manners as life habits that show respect. **Teach** your child to say please and thank you as soon as he can talk. If he asks for something, have him try to say please before you give it. Then, when he takes the object, have him repeat "thank you." **Teach** him to say "no thank you" rather than just "NO." (The people at the park we visit are amused by my son's use of manners. When it is time to leave, and I start to take him home, my son says "No thank you mamma, no thank you.") **Teach** your child that the consequence of using good manners is good relations with others.

Teach a school age child to open doors for his elders, and to treat people his grandparent's age with special respect. Show him how to greet others appropriately. Discourage him from racing to be at the front of the line. He can let others go first. Reinforce these lessons your child will also learn in school. Make it a point to check in with your child's teacher regarding his behavior. Expect your child to respect the authority of his teacher and other school officials. Unless there is some extraordinary circumstance, support the judgments of the adults that are responsible for teaching your child.

Lack of respect for personal boundaries is another sign of a dominance drive out of control. Personal boundaries include: keeping ones body acceptably clean and covered, keeping a respectful distance between oneself and another, knocking before entering another's space, and keeping hands off another's belongings. Beginning as early as possible, teach respect for personal boundaries.

Modesty is a virtue not acknowledged by the popular culture. Modesty is respect manifested in dress and personal appearance. Children should show respect for others by maintaining personal grooming and hygiene. **Teach** your child to keep his private parts covered. Clothing is the most basic boundary we place between others and ourselves. Therefore, good boundaries begin with appropriate dress. Likewise, **teach** your child to honor the modesty of others by exercising restraint over his curiosity.

Impulse Control, Moral Values and Having Fun

Next to eating chocolate cake, having sex and social power are two of the most pleasurable sensations humans experience. In fact, these two are so enjoyable that many of our other pleasurable experiences pale in comparison. The time between 5 and 11 years of age is a unique period in the life of a person. During these years, a person has fewer of the impulses that come from the sex drive and the need for social dominance.

It is important for children of this age group to learn to enjoy many different activities, including, intellectual learning, physical exercise, art and music. Children should also develop an appreciation for the beauty of nature and learn to enjoy friendships. Children who learn to enjoy these things prior to puberty are in a good position to have proper balance in their lives later on (see Balance in Pleasure, p. 144).

Adolescents who have a wide range of interests are less likely to be overwhelmed by peer pressure and sexuality. Adolescents who enjoy many different things are also less likely to believe that adults who impose rules on their behavior with their friends are taking away all their fun. These teens have an easier time with morality because they do not view morality as a burden.

Think about all the moral values you hold dear. Keep in mind that if you want your child to have the same values, you will have to **model** and **teach** them. Your spiritual community, his scout troop, athletic coaches and teachers will all be your allies as you raise your child. The popular culture, television and some of your child's peers may be your enemy. Make sure you and your child are surrounded by positive **influences**.

Moral Values that Immunize Against Antisocial Personality Traits and Addiction

Moral values that immunize against antisocial personality traits and addiction fall into three general categories. These categories are values regarding the Self, values regarding others, and values regarding society. A full intellectual and emotional understanding of these moral values develops in steps over the first fifteen years of life. However, begin **teaching** the rules very early. That your child does not understand fully the purpose of the rules is not a reason to delay **teaching**. Remember, in addition to **teaching** these values you will have to **model** them. You should also surround your child with positive **influences**.

Moral Values Regarding the Self

♥ LOVE YOURSELF–take care of yourself. Loving yourself means taking care of yourself. Treat your body well, exercise, eat right and keep yourself clean. DO NOT TAKE UNNECESSARY RISKS WITH YOURSELF.

♥ LOVE YOURSELF–learn impulse control. When a

parent loves a child, he teaches that child to control himself. A child who truly loves himself learns impulse control. He practices impulse control because he knows that over gratification of the basic drives is harmful. SELF INDULGENCE IS NOT THE SAME AS SELF LOVE.

♥ LOVE YOURSELF–do your best work. Take pride in who you are by doing the best you can and taking credit for the good that you do.

♥ LOVE YOURSELF–believe in a higher purpose for your life. Belief in a higher purpose for life acts as an immunization against substance abuse, and early sexuality. Without a strong belief in a higher purpose, there is no reason not to pursue gratification of impulses. Belief in a higher purpose for life does not necessarily have to involve belief in God. Even if you don't believe in God, you can still believe in a higher purpose for your own life and the lives of your children. Help your child discover his own special purpose **As humans, we do not have to be mastered by any of our drives. We can build, we can create, and we can make our world a better place.**

Moral Values Regarding Others

♥ LOVE YOUR NEIGHBOR–take care of your neighbor. Loving means caretaking. Look out for others when you can. Care for those in your own family first.

♥ LOVE YOUR NEIGHBOR–control your impulses. Love means not exploiting your neighbor by lying to him, cheating him or stealing from him.

Moral Values Regarding Society

♥ LOVE YOUR COMMUNITY–take care of your community. Loving caretaking extends to your community. Show your love of community by abiding by rules and laws and taking care of the environment.

Reaching for the Stars

Develop your own list of valued personal qualities. Search among friends, books and media for individuals who **model** these qualities. Talk to your child using these models as examples. Share books together. Reward your child for associating with friends who are polite, respectful and achieving in school. Discourage associations with disrespectful, misbehaving children. A bad peer group can undo years of hard work.

Get to know your own child. What does he enjoy? What does he do well? If he is good at sports, he can develop leadership skills by becoming Captain of his team. He can invite less gifted friends for practice sessions. If your child is bright, artistic, musically or mechanically inclined, help him develop himself. **At risk** children may also be especially charismatic and outgoing. **Teach** that we all have the responsibility to be the best we can be. **Those who have been blessed with special abilities must develop them and use them to make the world a better place.**

If your genetically **at risk** child is ten years old or more and seems to be stuck at moral development Stage 0, you need to get professional help right away. If he is under 10 and showing no signs of puberty, start working on the problem yourself and get help. A ten year old, heading toward puberty who operates by the "I should get my own way" principle and has problems with obedience, will have even more problems later.

If you are having trouble parenting him now, your troubles will likely get worse. (See Chapter 11 for advice on getting the most help from professionals.)

CHAPTER 6

THE INNER TRIANGLE REVISITED

Summary Of Possible Genetically-Determined Inborn Qualities Important In Antisocial Personality Disorder And Addiction

Inborn Attribute	Definition
Aloof	Difficulty forming and enjoying attachments
Impulsive	Defective impulse control
Fearless	Lack of fear
Outgoing	Strong desire to explore social and physical environment
Dominant	Strong desire to be at the top of the pecking order
Anger-Prone	"Hair-trigger" for anger

The chart on page 166 displays a list of possible genetically determined inborn qualities important in the development of antisocial personality disorder, addiction and ADHD. At first glance, these qualities may seem opposed to one another. For example, how can a person be aloof, socially outgoing and socially dominant? These qualities do precisely describe a person with antisocial personality disorder. Although these individuals do not love others in the usual sense, they do not like to be alone. They have a strong desire to explore the social environment, and have a strong desire to achieve social dominance. Since they lack the **ability to love** and **moral reasoning ability**, the sky is the limit when it comes to techniques employed to gain the strongly desired social dominance.

Just how then, does antisocial personality disorder develop? Scientists still do not know exactly how antisocial personality develops. However, the current literature suggests that antisocial personality disorder begins to develop very early in life as the child's natural aloofness and his drive to explore the environment add to create a habit of emotional distance from parents. This distance is magnified by the child's fearlessness, as he doesn't feel a great need for parental support. Fearlessness and the lack of a strong bond with parents prevent the development of conscience, which usually occurs prior to age five.

The child prone to antisocial personality disorder also has unusually strong drives. These drives go unchecked due to lack of conscience, poor impulse control and due to continued inadequacies in the parent-child relationship. The elementary school aged child never develops a sense of mastery over his drives and emotions. **Instead, his drives and anger rule his behavior.** With sexual development, the very powerful drives for sexuality and social dominance fully emerge. The child already has no conscience, and does not practice good impulse control. The love of his parents has little or no influence over him. Therefore, as an adult, his very powerful drives continue to determine ALL of his behavior.

Lesser (or perhaps different) forms of antisocial personality disorder can develop if the parent-child bond is weak rather than nonexistent, and if impulse control is weak rather than severely impaired. Remember that the parent-child bond needs to be strong for the entire first 15 years of a child's life– if he is to develop properly. The parent-child relationship must grow and change along with the child. Parental training of **impulse control** must be consistent throughout childhood, and, most importantly, during the time of transition from child to teen. Finally, in order to prevent antisocial personality traits, children must be taught moral values. Trauma and association with emotionally callous peers can erode away the effects of positive parental influence. Teens and adults with antisocial personality traits are very prone to addiction.

A Story With A Happy Ending

The inborn qualities that are a set up for antisocial personality disorder and addiction can also be a recipe for success.[88] Fearless, driven, outgoing people tend to be likable and entertaining. When combined with ability to love, a degree of impulse control, moral reasoning ability, and intelligence, these qualities make an individual capable of great leadership. Many of our favorite politicians (of both parties) occasionally get in trouble due to lapses in **impulse control**. This is no coincidence; they have very powerful drives!

On a visit to a local park, I met a man who demonstrated these qualities. He was a grandfather of two boys who played with my son. The man had come to the park with his daughter-in-law, the mother of the boys, and a friend of mine. In telling his story, the man said, "I was too young for Korea and too old for Vietnam." He was energetic, vigorous and charming. We had the usual conversation that takes place between people whose lives center on their kids. He said he was glad to have raised two boys and now to have two grandsons. "Boys are easier because they're not as into feelings." "They are more straight forward." With these statements, he indicated that he wasn't completely comfortable with the feeling realm.

He also talked about his earlier life. He had been born and raised in our area. He was a star athlete and had devoted himself to coaching youth sports. "I was good at coaching because I remembered what it was like to be a 16 year old boy. One minute you want to be on your mommy's lap, the next minute you want your freedom and to chase girls." He talked about the rather wild life he led in his youth. To this day, he described himself as enjoying gambling. He left me with the impression that **impulse control** was something he had to work to achieve. He was very driven both to accomplish and to gratify his impulses.

On the other hand, the man had rather strong **moral reasoning ability**. He held strongly to the moral values he believed in. He had been married 40 years to the same woman and described himself as still being "in love." He worked hard, as he had successfully owned and prospered two businesses. Most interesting, was that he had served our country abroad as part of the Foreign Service. His likability, outgoing attitude and good people skills made it easy for him to relate to people of many different cultures. He had lived in Europe and the Middle East.

He talked about how our community had changed since the time he grew up. He said that the social bonds were much stronger back then. "There was no TV, and we all played together." "No one would have stolen a child out of my neighborhood." "Everyone watched out for each other." I wondered how different this man's life would have been had he been born and raised in today's world.

The Sides of the Inner Triangle

A person is defined by his **ability to love. Ability to love** forms the base of the inner triangle. **Impulse control** is essential for life in society. **Moral reasoning ability** makes a person "good." As you read the preceding chapters, I am sure you realized all three grow together. Furthermore, the growth of one side of the triangle encourages the growth of the other two sides. The development of **impulse control** makes a child easier to love, and more receptive to parental love. Love between parent and child gives the child incentive to learn **impulse control**. Love also encourages a child to adopt his parent's moral values. **Impulse control** enables a child to conform his behavior to the moral values he has learned. The triangle is only a construct that can help us visualize these relationships.

Is there scientific evidence for a relationship between the development of the **ability to love** and the development of **impulse control** and **moral reasoning ability**? Several studies have directly demonstrated a relationship between **ability to love** and **impulse control**. Across cultures, mothers that provide warmth and physical comfort to their infants have more obedient, less impulsive toddlers.[89] When mothers and toddlers have a pattern of sharing love, the toddlers develop into moral preschoolers.[90] Love between mothers and toddlers also predicts later ability to understand feelings.[91] The love relationship is more important for the development of **impulse control** and **moral reasoning ability** than is a strict parental style. Mothers who rely on punishment to control behavior have less well-behaved children.

When there is a close love relationship between parents and children, children enjoy their parents and want to stay in their good graces. Parents are also more likely to talk about feelings and moral principles when there is a close loving relationship. Children respond best to parents who **teach** by talking to them. Studies show that when loving parents talk about feelings, behavior and morality, children listen. *Love turns children into sponges ready to absorb the lessons parents teach.*

Imagine the most difficult job you have ever done, a job that took 100% of your effort. That job is what some children face when it comes to learning **impulse control**. A child born with below average **impulse control** has a terrible time and deserves our understanding. He does things sometimes even before he realizes what he has done. Studies show that the most loving successful parents actually protect their children from entering into situations they aren't capable of handling. They set their children up for success![92]

Now imagine what it will take to motivate a child to work hard at improving **impulse control**. We all know intuitively that love is the only real motivation. Love and trust between parent and child make for a child that is eager to please his parent. The motivation for good behavior is getting is more love, not avoiding punishment. A child that is eager to please will work at **impulse control**. In fact, a solid parent-child bond predicts good **impulse control**.[93] **Trying to instill fear of physical punishment does not help at risk children, partly because at risk children do not have a normal fear response.** Studies show that punishment is also a less effective means of teaching moral values. Fear of punishment may cause children to behave in a good way when adults are watching but does not extend good behavior into unsupervised situations.

It is as if a child must have a very strong memory (both visual and verbal) of his parent within himself in order to have a conscience. The image/memory will not be powerful unless there is a strong positive love relationship. This love relationship gives the parent such **significance** to the child that the parent actually becomes part of the child's developing *Self.*

The Points of the Inner Triangle

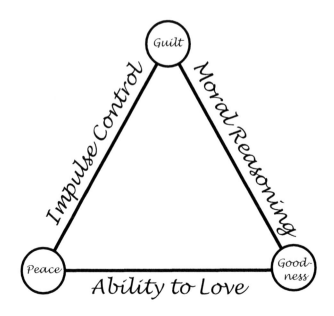

Do the points of the inner triangle have any meaning? I think they do. Consider the point where **ability to love** meets **impulse control**. The intersection of these two determines our capacity for inner peace. Inner peace can only be realized through moderation of impulses and quality attachments with others. True goodness lives where **ability to love** and **moral reasoning ability** meet. A loving, moral person is truly good. The conscience resides at the intersection between **impulse control** and **moral reasoning ability**. The amount of guilt a "normal" person lives with is directly determined by his ability to control his impulses in line with his moral beliefs.

Those with antisocial personality disorder lack guilt and experience other emotions differently than the rest of us. Guilt is a feeling which likely develops as an extension of the fear response. The fear that develops into guilt, is both that of losing the approval of the parent and of incurring punishment. Since some **at risk** children have a weak relationship with their parents and a defective fear of punishment, they have a difficult time developing guilt. This is why gently encouraging the fear response in **at risk** children is important (pp. 120-126).

Think again about how fears are extinguished. They are extinguished when feared stimuli are associated with pleasurable stimuli. How then can a parent be both a source of pleasure (the reward of love) and fear? A parent who chooses to exert his authority through causing fear, loses when it comes to being a source of pleasure. The fear that leads to the development of guilt cannot be fear of the parent himself. It has to be fear of losing the parent's approval. The only way a child can fear losing the parent's approval is through a loving relationship. **Guilt develops as an extension of fear of separation from the parent.**

Let us go back to discussing inborn or genetic vulnerabilities and critical periods again. A child born with the ability to easily attach to his parent will have an easy time developing guilt. If attachment is strong, there is distress at separation. With time, the distress at separation becomes distress at threatened separation. Distress at threatened separation allows for the development of guilt.

(Remember the story of my son and the dreaded dark place!)

What about the child born aloof? The child born aloof has a difficult time forming and enjoying attachments. He is more interested in mastering his environment and achieving social dominance, and is rather disinterested in attachment to his parent. His distress at separation is fairly low, as he can move on to exploration and mastery in the parent's absence. This child has a difficult time developing guilt. **Parenting the aloof child requires an extra focus on maintaining the importance of the love relationship.**

We all know that there is a critical period for this strong attachment to parent. Children only become distressed at separation from parents when they are young. Maturation involves becoming less distressed by parental separation. This is why there is a critical period for developing the capacity for guilt. Development of guilt depends on distress at separation, and most children grow out of the distress.

Environmentally-Induced Antisocial Personality Disorder

What kinds of early experiences cause antisocial personality disorder in children with little or no genetic risk? I have already indicated that brain injury can cause antisocial personality disorder. That is why birth trauma and prenatal exposure to cigarette smoke place a child at risk. The parts of the brain that mediate fear and appreciation of consequences may be especially sensitive to injury.

Research regarding the bond between a child and his primary care giver clearly demonstrates that the presence of a good early attachment is protective against antisocial personality disorder. Absence of a secure early attachment places a child at risk. This risk is greatly increased when the child is also a victim of physical or sexual abuse. Abuse at the hands of a parent who is supposed to love and care for the child, is emotionally devastating. Remember that learning to love involves having the habit of enjoying parents. How can a child enjoy his tormentor? (Children whose parents abuse them sometimes stay sane by having imaginary parents they love and enjoy. Isn't the human mind amazing?)

It is important that parents not torment their children with emotional or physical abuse. There is a clear distinction between limit setting and abuse. Limit setting done in the manner I have described in this book, empowers a child to gain **impulse control. Abuse destroys his spirit and ability to love.**

Severe trauma like physical or sexual abuse can also cancel out the protective effects of secure early attachment. The older a child gets, the smaller the observed positive effect of good early attachment becomes as older children have had more time on this earth to experience trauma.[94] It is therefore vitally important that children be protected from the effects of trauma. (See "Guiding Your Child in the Midst of Tragedy" p. 82 of this book.)

Lack of limit setting by parents can also cause antisocial personality traits in children who had good relationships with caregivers early on and no genetic predisposition. Some parents are good at caring for infants and young children, but have difficulty with older children. A parent must grow and change as his child develops and his needs change. Parents must be **responsive** to their child's needs in each developmental stage. **Children need discipline and correction as well as cuddling and praise.**

A child with a history of good early attachment to his parents, who is later neglected, will turn to peers to fill the void. Generally, this results in antisocial behavior since as a group the children then seek unrestrained gratification of drives. Engaging in antisocial behavior with peers that is exploitative of others serves to make children even more callous and to impair **ability to love.**

The Other Side of the Coin

In this book, I have addressed the issues involved in raising an outgoing, fearless, impulsive child who desires to be socially dominant. I have not addressed the other side of the coin. There are children who are born introverted, timid, controlled and submissive. There are also introverted children with poor **impulse control** in some areas. These children are also at risk for problems as adults. For example, children who are excessively timid and shy are at risk for anxiety disorders. Anxiety and mood disorders also increase risk for addiction. If your child is gentle, shy and timid, you can be reasonably certain he will not develop antisocial personality disorder.

Responsiveness is the key to parenting any child. Parents of timid children must customize parenting practices to meet the needs of these children. Timid children may not need as much structure as fearless children. Instead, they need encouragement to be more adventuresome. Regardless of inborn temperament, all children need loving parents who are dedicated toward helping them realize their full potential.

Illness or Evil?

If antisocial personality disorder is an incurable condition that develops as a result of an interplay between genetics and early environment, is it right to hold affected people accountable for their actions? This question has been answered by our legal system. Adult psychopaths are considered responsible for their own behavior. What about a 14-year-old psychopath? Is he responsible for his own behavior that results from powerful impulses? Our legal system tends to hold even 14-year-olds accountable for the serious crimes they commit. This approach is a pragmatic one. If society were to stop holding psychopaths responsible for their behavior, what would we do with them?

With the recent advances in the scientific understanding of behavior and the decline of the guiding force of religious institutions, many people are confused about the concept of evil. If psychopaths are suffering from a developmental disorder, how can they be evil? In answering this question for myself, I have decided that the same pragmatic approach is best. I have come to believe that an evil person is one who exploits or harms everyone or most everyone he/

she encounters. There are many, many more evil people in the world than the ones we hear about on the news. At least eight million evil people live camouflaged in our American society. I can personally attest to the fact that these evil people exist! The illness question does not really matter to me at this point, since there is no effective treatment for antisocial personality disorder. Although I feel pity for those with antisocial personality (and addiction), I nonetheless recognize that they can be very dangerous.

Speaking as an armchair philosopher, I think that when we study antisocial personality disorder and how it develops, we are actually studying the means by which evil enters our world. Since we are physical beings, living in a physical world, evil has to be a physical condition. Is there any evil that is not caused by some combination of callousness, poor impulse control and faulty moral reasoning? If through more effective parenting practices, we were able to reduce the prevalence of antisocial personality traits and addiction in our society, the effect would be a reduction in the amount of evil in the world.

CHAPTER 7

ADDICTION REVISITED

How Does Addiction Happen?

Addiction is a terrible yet amazing affliction. Addiction means the pursuit of intoxication with a substance at the expense of everything and everyone in the addict's life. This behavior is truly baffling. How can it be that intoxication can become the single most important thing in a person's life? The personal, tragic story of addiction is unfortunately all too common in America. Every year, many addicts die diseased, alone and penniless in the streets.

Addiction starts with an impulse. The impulse is to use a substance for entertainment. People that are prone to addiction generally have a hard time enjoying little things and often feel bored.[95] (Remember, what I said about balance in pleasure in chapters 4 and 5). This boredom causes them to take risks seeking pleasure and entertainment.

Once an addiction-prone person tries a substance of abuse, he is hooked. Substances of abuse exert more powerful effects on people who are prone to addiction. Those prone to addiction have dysfunction in the parts of the brain that perceive reward and tell us to avoid punishment.[96]

There are many studies showing that addiction-prone people have brain dysfunction and a different brain chemistry. Just as for antisocial personality disorder, the problems in brain chemistry and function that cause addiction result from BOTH genetics and childhood experience. When parents fail to teach impulse control, enjoyment of simple things, pride in personal accomplishment and a higher purpose for human life, a genetically **at risk** child develops a chemical as well as spiritual imbalance. The nature of this chemical imbalance and brain dysfunction in addiction is not yet fully understood and may be different for different addicts. **The important point is that parenting affects the structure, function and chemistry of the child's brain.**

Like those with antisocial personality disorder, individuals prone to addiction also respond poorly to punishment.[97] They thus have a difficult time appreciating the negative consequences of substance abuse. For example, many people who drink too much alcohol have a hangover the next day. This hangover is unpleasant (punishing) and discourages the person from drinking too much again. Similarly, the after effect of cocaine is profound depression in most people. This depression makes many people who try the drug only try it once. Addiction-prone users quickly forget the pain they go through when the drugs they use wear off. They also are not truly "punished" by the negative consequences of addiction. Being diseased, alone and penniless doesn't always make them stop using.

Lastly, addiction-prone individuals also have to have a large sense of entitlement. Addicts feel entitled to use substances at everyone else's expense. It is commonly known that many addicts feel entitled to drive under the influence, and that pregnant addicts feel entitled to expose their unborn to dangerous substances. Addicts generally do not believe they are obligated to anyone else. Instead, they believe everyone else is obligated to support their need for intoxication.

The sense of entitlement addicts have is related to impaired **ability to love** and is a trait developed during childhood. The impairment in **ability to love** and resulting sense of entitlement, is amplified greatly by the over use of addictive substances. Addictive substances are so rewarding to the addict, that any joy he feels from intimate, loving empathetic relationships pales in comparison to the joy of intoxication. Attachments, devoid of joy, become expendable. Any empathy the addict feels is quenched by the callousness that occurs from exploiting others to obtain substances.

In summary, addiction is caused by impairment of all three sides of the Inner Triangle. Impairment in **ability to love**, **impulse control** and **moral reasoning** together set a person up for addiction should he try an addictive substance. There are two parts to not becoming an addict. *Never try a substance of abuse and develop fully into a loving, caring person with a wide range of interests, morals, and impulse control.*

If Alcohol Abuse Is in Your Child's Genes

"A child who reaches age 21 without smoking, abusing alcohol or using drugs is virtually certain never to do so."- Joseph A. Califano, Jr., Chairman and President, The National Center on Addiction and Substance Abuse at Columbia University. Adolescents who begin drinking before age 15 are four times more likely to develop alcohol dependence than those who begin drinking at age 21. The average age when kids first taste alcohol is 11 years for boys and 13 years for girls. The average age at which American teen*s begin* drinking **regularly** is 15.9 years old. If your genetically **at risk** child does what most other kids are doing, he will likely destroy his life!

If you are with me raising an **at risk** child you cannot look to the behavior of your family, friends and neighbors then set your standards. YOU HAVE TO BE DIFFERENT. Remember, **model**, **teach**, **influence** is your motto. **Model** for your child how to have fun without alcohol. Do not have alcohol present at every party or get together. Limit your association with friends who need to use alcohol in order to have fun. **Teach** your child that a problem with alcohol is in his genes, and he should NEVER drink. Your child cannot experiment because he will not be able to erase the bad results if his experiment goes wrong. **Influence** your child for the better by not keeping alcohol in the house. Closely supervise his social activities make sure there is no alcohol present at the parties he attends. I know that my suggestions may seem difficult and extreme, but science has no better advice to offer regarding how to prevent alcoholism.

A Path Into Addiction

Nick is a good-looking kid. He tends to be energetic and have a hard time sitting through classes but because he is very bright, he always did well in school. He is now 16, addicted to heroin and contemplating dropping out of school. Nick's parents are both successful. Nick's grandfather on his mother's side was alcoholic and Nick's mother coped by over achieving. She has an MBA and is Vice President at her company. Nick's father is an attorney.

Nick's parents divorced when he was 11 and he never really got over the pain. Initially, Nick saw his father every weekend. As Nick got older, he complained that visitation interfered with his social life. Visitation became less and now he rarely sees his father. Because of his pain over the loss of his family and relationship with his father, Nick doesn't really enjoy much. He was always the class clown and so was well liked but wasn't emotionally close to anyone.

When Nick was small, he spent time with both his parents who loved him and taught him their values. But, Nick's parents didn't really place a value on impulse control. They felt Nick should be "happy" and "free to express himself." Neither of his parents is particularly religious or spiritual. Nick has every thing a boy his age could want including a new car. That is why his mother can't understand why things went so wrong.

When he was 14, Nick met Sara while walking down his street. She had just moved into the neighborhood. Sara was 15, pretty, and into experimenting with sex and substances. Initially, Nick was only curious about Sara. Then, after spending time and having relations with her, he felt a connection he didn't have with anyone else. Sara and drugs filled the emptiness Nick felt.

Nick's parents were shocked when his grades declined last year. They thought Nick seemed "happier" than he had for a long time. Since Nick had Sara to talk with, he stopped taking to his mother. His mother didn't notice because she had been working on a new project at work. Nick told his parents that his grades dropped because school got harder. His parents hired a tutor, not suspecting there were deeper issues.

Nick's life illustrates the way trauma and other factors including serendipity interact in a child's life. Nick's poor relationship with his parents, poor **impulse control** and under-developed value system set him up to try drugs and become addicted. Once Nick gave into his sexual impulses and the impulse to try drugs, he was lost. These were only a temporary fix for the pain he carried in his life, but since he is genetically predisposed to addiction, once he tried drugs he could not stop. Nick's peer group also deteriorated because "good" kids who found out about his behavior refused to associate with him. Nick "hung out" with other kids with substance abuse issues and tried many different drugs before he found heroin, his drug of choice.

Nick's path into addiction began when his parents failed to teach him the value of **impulse control**, and with the way they handled the trauma of the divorce. Since neither of Nick's parents had a close relationship with him, they were both unaware of his struggles. Nick's impulses got the better of him when it came to Sara and using drugs.

Nick's **moral reasoning ability** was also not advanced enough to provide him with the tools to cope with either his feelings of emptiness or with temptation. His parents hadn't provided him with a sense of a real purpose for life. That was because his parents didn't really believe in a purpose themselves. When Nick met Sara, he didn't see anything wrong with just trying to have a good time. We all lost out when Nick became an addict. Nick could have been someone who did a great deal of good for others.

Recovery

Recovery is the process of overcoming addiction. The point I wish to make is that recovery involves restoring the Inner Triangle. When antisocial personality disorder and addiction coexist, there is a bad prognosis for the treatment of addiction.[98] In my opinion, the reason is that the person with antisocial personality disorder has irreparable defects in all three sides of the Inner Triangle.

Every person in recovery knows that recovery involves more than just stopping the use of substances. Alcoholics who stop drinking but do not recover are called "dry drunks." Dry drunks continue to have damaged **ability** to **love**, **impulse control** and **moral reasoning ability**. This damage prevents an affected person from living a fulfilled life and puts him at great risk for relapse.

An addicted person must work very hard to recover **ability to love**, **impulse control** and **moral reasoning**. The 12 steps of Alcoholics Anonymous are not only a path to "sanity," they are a path toward healing the Inner Triangle. Many of the 12 steps are about building **impulse control**. The first step, acknowledging the problem is labeling an impulse, as a parent should do for a child. The addict is also asked to acknowledge the very powerful effects the impulse to use has on his behavior. Other steps in the 12-step program serve to restore feelings, relationships and empathy. Contained within the 12 steps is the value of a higher purpose for living.

Addicts, like Nick in the story above, should have done recovery work *before becoming addicted*. However, the saying, "better late than never" is really true when it comes to recovery. The recovery process can make a person "better" than he otherwise would have been. The addict is especially challenged to make good out of his tragedy. Making good out of tragedy means developing greater **ability to love**, more **impulse control** and higher **moral reasoning** than existed prior to the addiction.

Predicting Recovery in Teens

The picture of a young person with addiction and signs of antisocial personality disorder is pretty bleak. Still, if your family is living with this tragedy, don't give up. Seek treatment for your son or daughter. A well-designed, well-executed study examined progression of substance abuse and antisocial behavior in teens who received substance abuse treatment.[99] The good news is that even in these very high-risk teens, progression to antisocial personality disorder only occurred in 61% of those studied. 39% did not go on to develop antisocial personality disorder. Progression to antisocial personality disorder was predicted by:

1. Onset of antisocial behavior prior to age 10.
2. More pervasive antisocial behavior.
3. More substance abuse.

The authors of this study suggest that teens at highest risk be selected for more intensive treatment of BOTH the underlying character problems and the substance abuse. Restoring the Inner Triangle by strengthening **ability to love**, **impulse control** and **moral reasoning** is the key to recovery.

CHAPTER 8

ADHD REVISITED

In the first Chapter I introduced the idea that ADHD is genetically transmitted and that ADHD, addiction and antisocial behavior occur together in some families. I have suggested in this book that poor **impulse control** forms part of the basis of the link between these three disorders.[100] What environmental factors cause poor **impulse control** and increase risk for ADHD? Smoking during pregnancy not only increases the risk for antisocial personality disorder, maternal smoking also increases risk for ADHD.[101] From studying the literature, I have come to the conclusion that the brain centers involved in **impulse control** may be very sensitive to environmental insult. This environmental insult could result from toxins (like cigarette smoke), vitamin deficiency, infectious diseases, and/or stress hormones. Stressful life events also increase risk for ADHD.[102] The increased risk for both ADHD and antisocial personality in males may be caused in part by the male brain having greater sensitivity to environmental insult.

Controversy surrounds the diagnosis of ADHD. Many wonder if the disorder even exists. There is also much concern over the use of stimulants for treatment of ADHD in children and adolescents. Even those that deny ADHD is a "true disorder," have to acknowledge the fact that there are some children who are disabled by inattention and impulsivity. When disability of any kind occurs during childhood, the danger is that development will be hampered and that the child will fail to reach his full potential.

Inattention can be academically disabling when a child fails to give close attention to details and makes careless mistakes in schoolwork. Inattentive children also have difficulty persisting in tasks; they shift aimlessly from one activity to the next, failing to experience the rewards associated with a job well done. **Perhaps worse, tasks that require sustained mental effort are experienced as painful and unpleasant to the inattentive child.**

Impulsivity is often socially disabling for children. Impulsive children interrupt others, become angry easily, intrude on peers, grab toys from friends, and clown around inappropriately. As mentioned in Chapter 4 impulsivity often leads to accidents and is a cause of physical injury in children with ADHD.

The disabling inattention and impulsivity seen in some children results from dysfunction in the brain and is due to both genetic and environmental causes. Recent studies have investigated the genetics of inattention and impulsivity in order to examine whether the two conditions are distinct or are manifestations of a common underlying problem. In favor of considering inattention and impulsivity to be separate conditions, girls with ADHD tend to be inattentive and have less problems with impulsivity.[103] However, the inattentive and impulsive subtypes of ADHD do not tend to breed true in families.[104] It therefore appears that inattention and impulsivity share a common cause[105] and that female gender may protect against impulsivity (perhaps by conferring resistance to environmental insult).

Since I am a physician, it is my bias to consider ADHD a legitimate disorder and to advocate for children with the disorder. In order to prevent complications and further disability, children with ADHD deserve appropriate diagnosis and treatment. Illness in a child is torment for his parents. ADHD is no exception. The parents of a child with ADHD worry about that child's physical, emotional, social and academic well-being. Parents also worry about what the

ADHD diagnosis says about how a child will function as an adult. This chapter will explore some of the worries of parents of children with ADHD.

Can ADHD be prevented?

Since genes are fixed at conception, most disorders with a genetic cause can only be prevented to the extent that there is also an environmental cause. Some researchers have suggested that the genetic component of ADHD can be as high as 90 per cent.[106] If these researchers are correct, prevention efforts in ADHD should be directed toward reducing symptoms and preventing complications of the disorder (secondary and tertiary prevention). On the other hand, environmental causes of ADHD may be operative in some families. Primary prevention of ADHD might be possible in these families. It is likely that reducing birth trauma, limiting exposure to toxins and providing an adequate diet early in life, would prevent ADHD in some children.

There are many studies (as discussed in Chapter 6) that show that a strong mother-child bond enhances **impulse control** in children. This strong mother-child bond results from physical, emotional and verbal intimacy between mother and baby/child. However, whether a certain kind of parenting could reduce the incidence of ADHD in families with a high genetic risk has not yet been studied.

Since parents can't wait for definitive studies before trying to help their children, I will put forth the following suggestions based on my best educated guess and a "do no harm" philosophy. If ADHD runs in your family, try to take special care of yourself during pregnancy. Certainly don't drink alcohol or smoke and avoid exposure to second hand smoke. Talk to your obstetrician about good nutrition and minimizing trauma to your baby during birth. Provide your baby/child with good nutrition as recommended by your health care provider. Establish a strong loving bond with your baby by holding him often, stimulating him physically, and talking to him. Try to act as a buffer between your child and life stress as I suggested in Chapter 3. Place a value on **impulse control** in your family as I discussed in Chapter 4. If you do your best in these areas, I believe you have done everything humanly possible to prevent ADHD in your child.

Are all children with ADHD similar?

All children with ADHD are not alike. ADHD may have at least three different subtypes. Children with ADHD often have other disorders along with ADHD. These disorders can include mood disorders, anxiety disorders, learning disabilities, conduct disorder and oppositional defiant disorder. Remember that ADHD itself is associated with impairment in only one side of the Inner Triangle. Nevertheless, impairment in **impulse control** can have a negative effect on the development of empathy and conscience. Therefore, some but not ALL children with ADHD are at risk for addiction and antisocial personality.

My child has ADHD. How can I tell if he is receiving the appropriate treatment?

Appropriate treatment starts with a thorough evaluation. Make sure the person evaluating your child is trained in assessing mental disorders in children. If your child has academic problems, make sure he is assessed for learning disability. The goal of treatment of ADHD is to reduce the symptoms enough so that emotional, academic and social development can proceed "normally." Ask yourself how well your child is doing emotionally, socially and academically. Is he age-appropriate in these areas or is he falling progressively more behind in spite of treatment?

Many parents don't want to hear this but, the most effective treatment for true ADHD usually includes the right kind of medication.[107] Many well done scientific studies have shown that medication management is the most effective treatment for ADHD. Just as there are some passionate anti-medication voices in our popular culture, many of those who treat ADHD are equally passionate about children receiving scientifically proven treatment. My colleagues tell me time and time again, that children who are taken off medication due to media reports, immediately begin to fall behind in their development. Considering that the consequence of untreated ADHD may be life failure due to poor academic achievement, or addiction or antisocial personality, medication is justified as ADHD is not just a nuisance disorder.

Any treatment carries with it risks and benefits. If your child is taking medication, he should be carefully monitored for side effects. Any side effects should be understood in relationship to the benefit your child is receiving from the medication. If your child is little improved with medication then, any side effects would tend to make his overall condition worse. On the other hand, you may be willing to live with side effects if it is clear that the medication is helping your child.

My child has ADHD. How can I keep him physically safe?

The risk of physical injury in children with ADHD is related to impulsive risk taking. Not all children with ADHD are impulsive risk takers. As discussed in Section 4.7.4 it is important that parents educate impulsive risk takers about safety. Insist your child wear a helmet when riding a bicycle, skating or skate boarding. YOUR IMPULSIVE-RISK TAKER REQUIRES MORE PARENTAL SUPERVISION THAN OTHER CHILDREN HIS AGE.

My Child Has ADHD. How Can I Help Him Socially?

"Normal" peers often recognize that children with moderately severe ADHD are impaired. As stated above, impulsivity can be socially disabling. Impulsive children become angry easily, interrupt others, intrude on peers, grab toys from friends, and clown around inappropriately. ADHD can therefore impact your child socially in two different ways. First, your child may experience peer rejection.

Second, your child's circle of friends may consist solely of other children who are as disabled or who are more disabled than he is. Both association with troubled peers and rejection by more "normal" children have negative consequences for children with ADHD. Parents need to help their children cope with rejection and discourage too much association with troubled peers.

If your child is experiencing the pain of peer rejection due to his ADHD symptoms, discuss this issue with his health care provider. Improvement in social functioning should be a goal of treatment. Many children with ADHD have limited ability to understand the motivations and feelings of others. Laboratory studies show that some children with ADHD miss important social cues and consider fewer possible responses.[108]

Your child needs to have some friends with good social functioning to help him learn better social problem solving. Some impaired children are more likely to propose aggressive solutions to problems with peers. These aggressive solutions can involve verbal and/or physical intimidation of peers. Aggressive behavior produces more peer rejection and increases both isolation and association with other aggressive children. Therefore, your child could be negatively impacted by aggressive problem solving strategies he learns from impaired peers. Directly discourage your child from using aggressive problem solving strategies. These strategies will not gain him friends or influence.

Your child may lack appreciation for the impact his behavior has on others. For example, did the teacher make everyone come in for recess early because your child (among one or two others) failed to complete work or clowned around? The teacher may be hoping that peer pressure will motivate your child to control himself. However, there is a fine line between peer pressure and peer rejection, and your child may not be able to control himself. In one laboratory study, boys with ADHD were unable to control emotional displays even when given instruction and incentive to do so.[109] Your child's teacher may need to be cautioned against punishing the entire class for his behavior. Help your child to see that peers may want to like him for his good qualities but that they are also put off by some of the things he does.

My child has ADHD. How can I help him academically?

Academic achievement predicts good outcome for children. It is important that you place a value on education and **model** this value for your child. Talk to your child about the importance of learning and doing his best in school. If your child is struggling, have him evaluated for learning disabilities. Work with the school around an individualized educational plan for your child.

The home environment and after school activities can greatly affect how a child does in school. Make sure your child goes to bed early enough to get the sleep he needs. Limit the amount of time he spends watching TV. Get into the habit of going to the library to pick out books to read for pleasure.

Most children with ADHD really need help with organization.

Do not allow clutter to build up in your child's space. Help him keep his belongings organized. Insist that he take time out every day to organize his schoolwork. Have your child show you his work and reward him for neatness, completion and organization.

While some would say it is better to "lay off" and "he'll sink or swim on his own" when it comes to school work. A forgotten assignment or misplaced work can be a cause of poor grades. Instead of motivating a child, the punishment of poor grades can be discouraging and reduce motivation. **Children get motivated when they believe it is important to succeed and they believe they can succeed!** Children are bombarded by so much these days they really need a parent to help them keep everything straight. By spending your valuable time helping your child organize himself, you show him directly the importance of organization. You can "lay off" once he proves he can "swim" and not drown in the paper work.

My child has ADHD. Will medication further increase his risk for addiction?

The diagnosis of ADHD carries with it an increased risk of substance abuse for both boys and girls.[110] In this book, I have proposed that the reason for the increased risk of substance abuse in children with ADHD is impairment in the development of the **Inner Triangle**, caused by poor **impulse control**. If I am correct, effective treatment of ADHD even with stimulants, should reduce later substance abuse. Furthermore, substance abuse in children with ADHD should be most frequent in those that also have impaired **ability to love** and impaired **moral reasoning ability**.

There have now been many well designed, scientific studies of later substance abuse in children with ADHD. Some of these studies have also examined whether treatment with stimulant medication increases risk of substance abuse. These studies do show that children most at risk for substance abuse have antisocial disorders in addition to ADHD.[111] The overwhelming majority of studies (12:1) show that treatment of ADHD with stimulants either reduces or has no effect on risk for substance abuse.[112] If, after reading this, you are still struggling with a decision regarding medication for your child, I encourage you to read the literature for yourself. Do not read news reports or opinions of celebrities, read the scientific literature! IF your child truly suffers from ADHD, he should receive the appropriate treatment. This treatment will reduce the impact of the disorder on his life.

My child has ADHD. Is he at increased risk for antisocial personality disorder?

A child psychiatrist I greatly respect reviewed this book and expressed concern that parents of children with ADHD would read it and be scared unnecessarily about the risk of antisocial personality and addiction in their children. He has been in practice many years and can attest to the fact that **most children with ADHD both "grow out" of the disorder and become well functioning adults**. While it is true that most children with ADHD achieve a good adjustment with treatment, the diagnosis of ADHD does increase risk for substance abuse and antisocial behavior. Substance abuse is most common in ADHD teens that also have antisocial behavior. I will therefore review the studies linking ADHD with antisocial behavior, and provide some suggestions for parents regarding warning signs.

A high percentage of both girls (35% in one study) and boys (66% in one study) with ADHD also have oppositional defiant disorder (ODD). Conduct disorder (CD) occurred in 11% of girls with ADHD and 21% of boys with ADHD.[113] As discussed in Chapter 7, even children with antisocial disorders are likely to improve over time (these are the children most at risk). Progression to adult addiction and/or antisocial personality is most likely in children who have BOTH ADHD and ODD/CD. The most recognized experts in the field have suggested that ADHD with antisocial behavior is a separate disorder.[114] Support for the idea that ADHD with antisocial behavior is a separate disorder comes from laboratory studies of boys with ADHD with and without CD. Boys with ADHD and CD have a pattern of low autonomic arousal similar to that of adults with antisocial personality (p. 14). Boys with just ADHD have patterns similar to those of non-diagnosed boys.[115]

Just what is the rate of progression of childhood ADHD, CD only and ADHD+CD to adult antisocial personality disorder? Good data are only available for boys. Progression to antisocial personality disorder occurs in 12-25% of boys with ADHD, 54% in CD only boys, and 56% of ADHD+CD boys. It should be noted that the rates of antisocial personality in ADHD are significantly elevated above that of the general population. Therefore, ADHD does carry with it some increased risk for both antisocial personality disorder and criminal arrest.[116] Since a child with ADHD is **at risk** for antisocial personality disorder and addiction, I suggest that parents of children with ADHD focus on helping their children fully-develop **ability to love, impulse control** and **moral reasoning ability**.

CHAPTER 9

THE INNER TRIANGLE AND ABILITY TO PARENT

In this book I have presented guidelines regarding parenting the **at risk** child. It is naïve to believe that implementing these guidelines is easy for everyone Parenting ability is directly affected by a parent's **ability to love, impulse control,** and **moral reasoning ability.** Thankfully, parents DO NOT have to be perfect to be effective!

Does the Inner Triangle Affect Parenting Ability?

We see the effects of the Inner Triangle on parenting ability most in the extremes. People who are incapable of warmth and empathy, have a difficult time parenting, even if **impulse control** and **moral reasoning ability** are relatively intact. Neglect is common when **love ability** is impaired in a parent. Parents who lack empathy are also more likely to adopt an overly controlling, authoritarian parenting style (see below). However, the parenting behavior of parents with under-developed **ability to love** can improve with teaching and practice.

A parent with poor **impulse control** has little patience with his children. Poor **impulse control** leads to child abuse. Parents who lose patience are likely to criticize and berate their children. When pushed, impulsive parents become hitters. If you have not been blessed with good **impulse control,** make it a point to work on yourself. **You can improve your parenting ability if you try!** Try to figure out what kinds of situations get you frustrated. When you feel yourself becoming angry with your child, back off and count to ten. Counting will help you calm yourself down. Do not punish a child when you feel angry. This is a set up for abuse. Seek support for yourself. You will have more patience if you feel loved and supported.

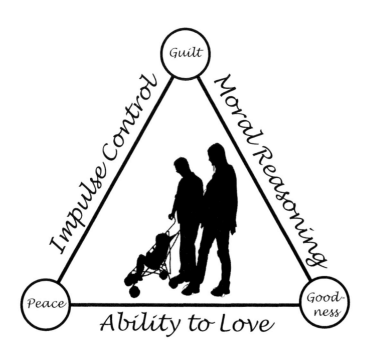

In some parents, poor **impulse control** means an out of control drive for social dominance. These parents feel an excessive need to dominate and control their children. These parents believe that it is their duty to rule with an iron hand. An excessive focus on social dominance in any relationship quenches love and affection. Parents who tend to be dominating can improve if they make an effort to be complementary of their children and spend time having fun with them.

When **moral reasoning ability** is under developed, parents fail to give their children a value system to live by. Since a human society is defined by its values, underdeveloped **moral reasoning ability** in parents leads to social decay. Look at the stages of development of moral reasoning. How far do you think you developed? Do you have a mission for your own life? Consider again the advice to connect with a place of worship or other spiritual community. Even adults need positive influences and a place where moral values can be reinforced.

Experts point out that we tend to raise our children the way we were raised. **Ability to love, impulse control** and **moral reasoning ability** are necessary qualities that affect parenting style. How developed these qualities are determines how a parent relates to his child. Interestingly, a parent's own parents were responsible for developing **love ability, impulse control** and **moral reasoning ability** in their child. Thus, the Inner Triangle tends to perpetuate its own dimensions from one generation to the next within families both through genetics and early learning. There is also selective mating within our population. This selective mating also perpetuates stability of Inner Triangle dimensions between generations both for better and for worse.

Take time out to assess the way you were raised. Were your parents warm and affectionate or rather distant? How much quality time did you spend together as a family? Is **ability to love** valued by your family of origin? How much are feelings discussed and processed? Did either one of your parents suffer from a mood disorder? Are your parents empathetic towards others? How do you think the way you were raised has affected your **ability to love**?

Did your parents model good **impulse control**? Were they consistent with discipline? Were your parents either controlling or overly permissive? Did your parents use spanking or yelling to discipline? Was sexuality discussed? How can you do better for your own child?

How advanced is **moral reasoning ability** in your parents? What are your parent's values? How much do you think you have been influenced by your parent's values? Do your parents act as though they believe in a higher purpose for living? How do you plan to help your child gain **moral reasoning ability** and a sense of a higher purpose for life?

Parenting Styles and Outcome for Children

Bossy Parents

Bossy (also called authoritarian) parents believe they must control their children through punishment that induces fear of the parent.[119] Studies show that these parental beliefs that exist even before a child is born, impair the development of empathy and morality in children.[120] Bossy parents do not understand that adopting the role of teacher is a much more effective way to assert parental authority. The word discipline is in the same family of words as the word disciple, or student. To discipline means to teach. "Discipline" that induces fear of the parent himself is harmful to children. Since bossy parents also believe that good parenting means controlling a child, they fail to teach the child to control himself.

Dominating, punitive parenting styles are associated with shame and poor outcome for troubled children.[117] Lengthy books have been written on the topic of shame. The point I wish to make is that shame is the feeling associated with being at the bottom rung of the social ladder. A parent who uses criticism or physical punishment to try to control behavior induces shame. **Shame is not a positive force in a child's life.**

If your child has that eagerness to please, but has poor **impulse control**, be careful how you discipline him. Think of the child with poor **impulse control** as disabled. Try to reward his efforts rather than punish him for his failures. You don't want him to become discouraged and give up, or develop anger toward you. Parents who are warm, **responsive** and who talk to their troubled children have better success with them over time.[118]

If your child is not eager to please, you must go back to square one and work on the relationship. You are like two lovers who have lost the romance and find themselves in a loveless marriage. You must romance your child anew. You must find the love you had for him on the day he was born. First, make a plan to spend more time with him. Consider this a lasting plan and not a temporary fix.

Picture your child in your mind. What are his good qualities? What do you love most about him? Work on keeping this "good" vision in your mind. Speak to your child in a more loving, complimentary tone. Hug and kiss him when the opportunity presents itself. Meet him where he is. Share activities he likes. Invite yourself into his world. Make him feel special. Your behavior toward your child should reflect the way you want your child to see himself.

Caretaking and Avoiding Servitude

As I sit writing, my son shouts "Juice!" I then say "May I please have some juice?" as I take a break to get him a drink. If my 12-year-old daughter came into the room and shouted "Juice!," she would get quite a different reaction. What happens between 2 and 12?

The answer is progressive independence. **The art of parenthood is caretaking without being a servant.** If I wait on a child that should be independent, I undermine my authority as a parent by assuming the role of his servant. I also fail to encourage enough independence. Conversely, if my 12 year old is sick, she may need me to get her some juice.

Pushover Parents

Pushover (also called permissive) parents have trouble with the concept of social dominance and authority. They tend to avoid asserting authority over their children and instead focus on the love relationship. The outcome of children of these kinds of parents depends on the child's temperament. Children who are shy, timid and intellectual may do well with pushover parents. A permissive approach will not work for the **at risk** child described in this book. Parental assertion of authority is required to help **at risk** children learn impulse control. **At risk** children develop anti-social personality traits when raised by pushover parents.

Why do pushover parents have such trouble asserting authority? Some people are just naturally less assertive than others are. Parents who are not good at self-assertion can improve if they focus on the limit setting techniques described in Chapter 4. Parents who are not naturally assertive should take extra care to be consistent with limit setting. Other parents have trouble asserting authority out of empathy for their children. Often, these parents had painful childhood experiences themselves. They remember what it was like to be a child at the mercy of unloving, punitive parents. If you are struggling with your own childhood memories, consider this: discipline at the hands of an unloving parent is very different from discipline that occurs as part of a love relationship between parent and child. The child disciplined by a loving parent may not like it, but, he knows deep down his parent is trying to help him.

Caretaking of children involves disciplining them. Parents should view discipline as stemming from parental duty rather than a need to dominate or control children. Sometimes it is hard for a loving parent to assume the role of disciplinarian. Love moderates the drive for social dominance. Have you ever noticed that many social animals spend hours grooming one another? Grooming is for more than cleanliness, it gives them a break from their dominance struggles, and so helps them to relax. It is difficult to switch back and forth between loving and asserting. While being loving is calming and relaxing, asserting is sometimes very stressful. Because asserting is stressful, some loving parents give up on discipline completely! These loving parents make the mistake of adopting an overly permissive parenting style. Remember, that a child left alone with his impulses is miserable. He needs his parents to teach him **impulse control**.

About Yelling and Spanking

Parents are confused by all the contradictory "expert advice" regarding yelling at children and spanking them. Is it possible to live with an active child and NEVER yell at him? and NEVER spank? I was pulling weeds in my yard and my 3-year-old daughter started to head for the street. Should I have yelled? "STOP!" or said, "Please dear don't go up to the road." If I hadn't yelled, my daughter might be dead!

There are two issues involved in the "discipline" of children. The first issue is that of training **impulse control**. I have already repeatedly stated that **at risk** children are unlikely to learn impulse control through yelling or physical punishment. Children are also masters of imitation. A child who learns that yelling and physical aggression are acceptable, will use these tools on his peers and family members.

The second issue in discipline is that of assertion of parental authority. (In other words, letting your child know that you are the boss.) Many social mammals use physical aggression to assert social dominance, should we humans do the same? Some authors have suggested that assertion of parental authority through spanking is "better than no assertion at all."[121] Is spanking really the only way to let a four-year-old know that you are the boss? It is not my intention to be sarcastic with these questions. Instead, I believe that parents who consider these issues as I have framed them will be able to come to their own conclusions.

Yelling should not be the first tool a parent uses to assert his authority. **Assuming the role of teacher is much more effective**. Children instinctively know that a parent who yells a lot is losing his grip. When you lose control, your child will perceive you as weak. If he perceives you as weak, he will not respect your authority.

Provoking Anger

"Do not provoke your children to anger."[122] Precious 2000-year-old parenting advice! The same writer urges us to use instruction and to encourage self-restraint in our children. A child who is chronically angry with his parent is prevented from gaining comfort from the love relationship. That relationship loses the "mutually responsive orientation" that is so important.

What do parents do to provoke anger in children? The answer varies according to the child's age but in general parenting styles that are inconsistent, overly demanding, and/or critical provoke anger. For young children, setting unreasonable limits or impossible demands, leads to anger. Young children need to be given reasonable limits that make sense. The more clear and consistent the rules are, the easier time children have conforming to them. Wouldn't you become frustrated if the rules changed in the middle of a game? Or, if the game was so difficult that you couldn't possibly win? A child of any age who is unable to gain the reward of pleasing his parent will become angry and finally disengage.

Teens and young adults also want to obtain the rewards of pleasing parents. The teen's reaction to constant parental criticism is anger. If your child or teen is having behavior or academic problems, do not allow the problems to define him or your relationship.   Label the behavior, label the problem, but do not label the child. Spending time having fun together is the key to not allowing problems to define your relationship.

Summary of Effective Parenting

- ♥ Effective parents are warm and empathetic.
- ♥ Effective parents reward good behavior.
- ♥ Effective parents establish clear rules and enforce them through limit setting.
- ♥ Effective parents model good behavior.
- ♥ Effective parents teach impulse control, respect and values.
- ♥ Effective parents surround their children with positive influences.
- ♥ Effective parents protect their children from entering into situations they won't be able to handle.
- ♥ Effective parents teach age appropriate life skills.
- ♥ Effective parents have fun with their children.

The Blame Game

Parents, especially mothers, have been blamed for the problems of their offspring since the beginning of psychiatry as a science. Is this blame well placed? In my opinion, when it comes to antisocial personality disorder, addiction and ADHD, there is plenty of blame to go around. Given the strength of the research findings, it is reasonable to blame genetics for these disorders. We can also blame poverty, the popular culture, society as a whole and perhaps the policies of our government.

The problem with blame is that it does not get us anywhere. Would it be just to punish the parents of psychopaths when they commit crimes? **While blame is not productive, taking responsibility is very productive**. If parents were to take the job of being parent very seriously, learn what science has to say about parenting and make raising children properly a top priority, then the problems of antisocial personality disorder and addiction in our society would go down. Parents need the support of everyone else in society to do this job.

In the beginning of this book, I alluded to the fact that I feel academic science has let parents down. While publishing articles that essentially blame mothers for not doing the job of mothering well, scientists and academics have done a poor job reaching out to mothers. They have also created such convoluted, confusing, long-winded, explanations for behavior that anyone hearing them speak wants to turn and run the other way! When it comes to understanding behavior, the simplest explanations are the best. **We humans are social creatures with a set of feelings and drives that determine behavior. We are born immature, and during the time we grow up, our brains are uniquely sensitive to being programmed to be social. Heredity determines how our brains receive programming instructions. If the programming does not happen properly, then function is impaired, perhaps for life.** Knowledge of these simple facts is really all that is needed to understand human behavior.

The job of parent is without question the most important job anyone does. Every job requires training and most also require mentoring. Mechanisms for training and mentoring of parents do not exist much in our communities. While high schools are required to teach students about sex, classes on human behavior that would prepare a teen to later assume the role of parent are not required! Does this make sense? Our culture lags painfully behind our scientific advances.

There are many, many studies demonstrating that when parents learn new parenting strategies, the behavior and well-being of children improve. **You don't have to undergo psychoanalysis, and you don't have to have a Ph.D. to learn the strategies!** Many of the studies of parent training have involved the highest risk, lowest income families. The training techniques involved employ the principles of love and discipline presented in this book. If training improves the chances of success for those at highest risk, it should be even more effective at reducing problems in other populations. **Most parents can do well with their children, if they learn how!**

The results of some of the studies of parent training are so striking that I will review a few of them here. In one study, low income mothers of at risk babies, received three counseling sessions when the babies were six to nine months of age.[123] The scientist spent these sessions educating the mothers regarding the importance of **responsiveness** and worked with them to figure out which soothing strategies worked best for each particular baby in question. Mothers were also encouraged to play with their babies, and given instruction in how to play. Babies of mothers who participated in these teaching sessions were later compared with a group of like babies of mothers who received no counseling. In this study, three individual counseling sessions made a big difference for mothers and babies. Sixty eight per cent of the babies of mothers who received counseling were independently rated as showing good attachment behavior at one year, compared with only twenty eight per cent of the comparison group.

Studies involving education of the parents of older children give similar results as the above study of infants. In one of these studies, mothers of a group of "difficult" 3-5 year olds received training on how best to **teach** their children. Mothers who learned good teaching techniques had significantly more compliant children than mothers who received no training.[124] Another study showed that nurse home visits of at risk mothers during pregnancy and through aged two, reduced incidents of running away, criminal arrest, and substance abuse when the children reached adolescence.[125] Another study addressed the effectiveness of parent training on Head Start children.[126] Children with the highest levels of conduct problems and mothers with the lowest parenting skills benefited most from the program. In another study,[127] researchers identified "at risk" children by participation in the WIC program. In this study, a motivational "check-up" interview and a few follow-up visits improved later behavior in boys.   What implication does all this research have for those who advocate *No Child Left Behind*?

Since religious institutions generally help people to think about a higher purpose for their lives, and help to promote family values, I believe scientists and academics do a disservice when they belittle religion. When I hear a scientist or academic bashing religion in the name of reason, I shudder. Has science really given us **A**nswers? Has science told us what the purpose of human life is? Science is more about asking questions, and solving problems, than giving **A**nswers.

While it is true that people fight over religion, especially these days, spirituality and belief are important for health– mental and physical. While the **ability to love** and good **impulse control**, are important, **moral reasoning ability** completes the inner triangle. **Moral reasoning ability** involves belief. Belief is an emotional connection to ideas. Humans are not logical robots. We feel, and feelings enter into the process of having belief in values.Psychopaths are an example of what happens when humans lack emotional connection with values and belief. Psychopaths can state the rules for appropriate behavior. However, because they do not believe in these rules the way the rest of us do, these rules do not guide their behavior. Scientists and academics should therefore not disparage our institutions of belief, they are very important to our well-being.

CHAPTER 10

QUESTIONS FROM PARENTS

Am I too late?

Do you worry that you are too late to save your child? Are you concerned he is too old for you to guide him to develop properly? Since antisocial personality traits can be prevented through primary prevention and reduced by secondary prevention, as long as there is a parent/child relationship there is hope. If a pre-adolescent school aged child has not developed guilt, there is still time to work on the relationship. If the parent can place himself in the center of that child's world, he can set the stage to become important enough to facilitate the development of conscience. If a child enjoys his parent's attention, he will respond emotionally to that parent's instruction and there is still time. To put it bluntly, if your child cares whether you are alive or dead, you can work with him. If he does not care, you need professional help to get him to care. Once he cares, he will be receptive to your teaching. The earlier you begin working on **love ability**, **impulse control** and **moral reasoning ability**, the better off you and your child will be.

Is it really possible to overcome inborn temperament?

The personality match between identical twins is not 100%. Similarly, "at risk" identical twins raised apart by non-relatives do not always share ADHD, addiction and/or antisocial personality disorder, even if one twin is strongly affected. Therefore, it has to be possible to mold personality beyond inborn temperament.

When scientists talk about risk, they speak of risk in a group of children that share certain characteristics. Statistics only apply to groups. Even experts cannot predict with certainty what will happen with any particular child. Statistics do help us to identify children that need special care and treatment.

Children born aloof and fearless can form secure attachments to their parents if parents provide unusually **responsive** care. While it appears that **impulse control** is to a large degree inborn, a child with less than average **impulse control** can improve. Better **impulse control** will only be possible if parent and child work at it. A child does not have to be at the mercy of an angry temperament. With practice, even angry children can learn to tone down their responses.

Parenting truly makes the difference for a child born challenged. Parents can allow inborn deficits to become real handicaps or they can encourage their children to be the best they can be. A child who makes small gains in **ability to love**, **impulse control** and **moral reasoning ability** every year may overcome inborn temperament completely by the time he reaches high school.

A small minority of children will develop disordered in spite of the best parenting and professional help. YOU WILL NOT KNOW IF YOUR CHILD IS IN THAT MINORITY UNTIL YOU HAVE GIVEN HIM THE BEST PARENTING AND PROFESSIONAL HELP AVAILABLE. If you have done your best as parent and your child still has problems, forgive yourself. Rest assured that his problems would be much worse if you had not done your best.

I just want my child to be happy. Is there anything wrong with that?

Yes, wanting "happiness" for your **at risk** child is not a good goal. Instead, work to help your child achieve well-being. There is a difference between happiness and well-being. Well-being comes from life habits that foster physical health, quality relationships and personal growth.[128] The job of obtaining well-being takes work! Doing the work may not make your child happy in the moment. Children whose parents focus on happiness rather than well-being become entitled, self-centered and spoiled.

My child is so oppositional I can't stand being around him. What do I do?

Is your child so oppositional that you feel you can't stand being around him? If you avoid him, he will be left alone to lose the struggle with his own impulses. Instead of giving up, try to find the "good" in your child and let the good be the meeting ground for your relationship. Does your child enjoy a hobby or professional sports? Share these interests with him on a regular basis. Tell him you are proud he has found an interest. Complement your child when you honestly can.

Maybe things have deteriorated so much that enjoying a meal or an ice cream together is all that is left. If that is what you have, enjoy the meal. Start there and get professional help. Do not expect immediate results. It can sometimes take months of working on a more positive relationship to chip away at the walls that have been built up.

Consider the possibility that there is something within you that is preventing you from fully loving your child. Perhaps your own early experiences, misplaced priorities or a draining adult relationship are the problem. I recommend you get therapy for yourself if you are having a hard time connecting with your child (See Chapter 3 for more on repairing broken relationships).

What about Diet and Allergies?

There is increasing interest in the effect of diet and allergies on behavior. I would contend that diet and allergies influence behavior by affecting **impulse control** (Chapter 4). This affect may be very significant in some children. The most obvious diet examples are caffeinated beverages and chocolate. A child made "hyper" by soda and chocolate has poor **impulse control**. It is not possible to train a child under the influence! Allergies make a child irritable and uncomfortable. A child itchy from eczema also has a hard time sitting still. Medications for allergies and asthma can also interfere with **impulse control**.

In my practice, I treated many parents who were searching for the "magic" diagnosis for their child. "If I could just figure out what is wrong with his diet, he would do better in school." "He's allergic to wheat, that's why he has no friends." Unfortunately, there are no quick or easy fixes for childhood behavior problems. While it is important to provide a healthy diet and vitamins to children and to diagnose allergies, the parent is still not off the hook. He must still focus on love and discipline. Very few children are "cured" through changes in diet alone.

My child's other parent who is an addict or has antisocial personality wants to see him. What do I do?

As adults, we can make choices for ourselves regarding whether or not to have close relationships with individuals with antisocial personality disorder and addiction. The underage sons, daughters, younger siblings, nieces, and nephews of these disordered people are all too young to understand the disorders that most adults cannot fully fathom. These children deserve to be protected. They are not capable of defining or weighing the consequences of a decision to share life with an addict or person with antisocial personality disorder.

Since your child is not capable of defining or weighing the consequences of a decision to share life with his other parent, you must do this job for him. Ask yourself if your child's other parent has a pattern of exploiting everyone in his life. If exploitation is the other parent's life-style, your child will also likely become a victim. The more attached a child is to an exploitative parent; the more he will be victimized (Chapter 12).

My child only seems to care for his friends. What do I do?

Children have intimacy needs just like adults. A child neglected by his parents will turn to peers to meet all his needs. Break this pattern by restoring your relationship with your child. See Chapter 3 for specific advice on how to restart your relationship with your child. Remember, a child age 11 or more may verbally tell you that he only likes his friends, while his behavior with you and at home says the opposite. Rely more on your own observations of your child than on his verbal reports.

There seem to be no nice friends for my child in our neighborhood. What do I do?

Your child should be kept away from peers who abuse substances or have callous antisocial behavior. This is true even if ALL of the other children in the neighborhood have these problems. Try to find structured activities for your child where he will be able to make friends outside your neighborhood. You may also need to consider other educational options for your child if he is unable to avoid negative influences at school. Many districts give the option of attending a Charter or Magnet school. These often provide better friends and better education. The earlier in life your child starts down the right path, the more likely he will be to stay on that path into adulthood.

I have a loving relationship with my child and he is still bossy and has poor impulse control. What do I do?

If you have a loving relationship with your child, you are in a good position to deal with any challenges that arise. Children are constantly growing and changing. A child's need for parental involvement and limit setting waxes and wanes in cycles. If your child suddenly seems to be struggling with bossiness and/or **impulse control**, reread Chapters 4 and 5 of this book, and then ask yourself the following questions:

1. Are bossiness and/or poor impulse control part of my child's temperament?
2. Is there some recent stress affecting my child?
3. Are there new peer influences in his life?
4. Is my child imitating some behavior he has seen at home?

Answering these questions will help you understand your child, and plan how to respond. Make a list of problem behaviors. Resolve in your mind to deal with them by communicating rules and imposing consequences consistently. **Do not worry that limit setting and imposing consequences will harm your relationship. On the contrary, proper discipline will improve your relationship! Teach** your child by talking to him calmly about his behavior and his need to exercise more control over his impulses. When you give your child feedback about his behavior, you send him the message that you are interested in him and care about him being a good person. "It seems you haven't wanted to listen to me lately. You haven't wanted to do you homework. You have to do your homework and listen to me even when you don't want to."

Do not expect immediate or even lasting results. Your job as parent is to do YOUR part. If you do your part well, your child will do his part better, but remember his part is to be a kid. You won't see the full results of having done your job well until your child is grown. Being a parent is exhausting work, and a thankless job!

My child treats me with disrespect. What do I do?

Remember, respect is an acknowledgement of the social dominance hierarchy. A child who treats his parents with disrespect rejects his parents' authority over him. Restoring respect involves reestablishing the dominance hierarchy within your family. A stable dominance hierarchy promotes the health and well-being of every member of the family. Stress occurs when there is uncertainty about who is in control. This stress causes increased levels of harmful hormones in those striving for control. Once the struggle is over, stress levels go down. Your child needs the security of knowing you are (and will remain) in control of the family. If he senses you are weak, he will be more likely to oppose you and draw you into a dominance struggle that is harmful to everyone in the family.

Establish your rightful place as head of your family by setting rules and imposing consequences. Also, do not forget that since you are the one in control of your family, it is your duty to take care of everyone else. Leaders take care of followers and receive respect in return. Taking care does not mean becoming a servant (p.198). Caretaking means looking after your child's well being. If you fail to perform the caretaking behaviors that go along with your status, your child will be inclined to oppose you as leader. Use contracts and limit setting to maintain your authority and show you care, avoid guilt trips and criticism.

How do I teach my child to handle the aggression other children may direct toward him?

Parents may be afraid that if they train their children to be relatively non-aggressive, their children will be handicapped when it comes to dealing with aggression others may direct toward them. This fear is to some degree realistic. Large, aggressive children are not the usual targets of bullies. The physical size, attractiveness, gender, and overall temperament of your child will influence the way other children respond to him. As a parent, you can help your child most if you appreciate his individual characteristics. Help your child understand the way other children view him and his behavior. Encourage him to do his best to develop into an attractive, sociable young person.

There are important parallels between the correct way for children to deal with aggression from other children, and the way adults deal with aggression from each other. As adults, we have laws that protect us from verbal and physical threats. The purpose of these laws is to protect us and prevent vigilante justice. If a neighbor repeatedly threatens, a responsible adult notifies the police. He does not take the law into his own hands and threaten his neighbor in return. Similarly, a child who is threatened should report the threats to parents and the appropriate authorities.

Teach your child to use rules and authority to deal with conflict.[129] Since there will always be people who are larger and more aggressive than your child, it is unlikely he could ever be aggressive enough to prevent aggression. Teach your child to avoid situations where he is likely to encounter aggressive children in an unsupervised setting. Remember, children are not capable of forming their own just society without adult input. Avoidance of potentially dangerous situations is sometimes very difficult because children do not want to feel left out. Prevent your child from feeling left out by providing him with many supervised opportunities for fun.

The best strategy for averting aggressive behavior, other than being large and aggressive, is to form strong alliances. If many good, close friends surround a child, he will be less likely to be bullied. Encourage your child to have a friend or two with him on his way to school, while at recess or on the schoolyard. Increasing **ability to love** by learning to be a good, loyal friend is a far better strategy for protection, than is being aggressive.

Cyberspace is the new meeting place for America's youth. Your child can spend the evening with a group of children in cyberspace, and if his computer is in his room, you wouldn't even know it. Teach your child that rules for appropriate behavior extend into cyberspace. Monitor who his online buddies are and do not allow him privacy until you are sure he can responsibly handle it. Many children have become deeply distressed and even suicidal over conversations that took place on the internet.

CHAPTER 11

HOW TO GET HELP FROM PROFESSIONALS

It is good for you to seek professional help and consultation for difficult parent/child problems. There are also many different kinds of professionals who offer help (Table below). Remember, a professional cannot take the place of you as parent. Furthermore, market forces and the government have allowed insurance companies to dictate the care that will be available to your family. The help you may really need is now so expensive that it may not be possible to get it. Thankfully, studies do show that when parents improve their parenting skills, children do better.

Since the expense involved in outpatient mental health care, rests primarily with the professional's time, you will be offered the bare minimum of face-to-face contact with the lowest level professional. There is also a nationwide shortage of child psychiatrists. The least expensive treatment is for a physician to see you for 30 minutes, write a prescription and have you return every 2-4 weeks for 15 minute follow up medication management visits. If you are lucky, you will be offered sessions with a therapist in addition to physician visits. In this system you may see an APRN, pediatrician, or psychiatrist for medication management and a MFCC, MSW or psychologist for therapy. You may have to give the same information to many different people. Some patients find it annoying to tell their stories over and over to different professionals who may not communicate well with one another.

PROFESSIONAL	EDUCATION AND TRAINING	WHAT THEY DO
Marriage and Family Counselor (MFCC)	College degree in Counseling	Counseling and Therapy
Social Worker (MSW)	4-year college degree +Masters degree in Social Work.	Counseling and Therapy
Advanced Practice Nurse (APRN)	4-year college degree in nursing + specialized training	Counseling and medication management
Child Psychologist (Ph.D.)	4-year college degree+ Ph.D. (Usually an additional 4 years) + internship	Behavior therapy, and Counseling, Psychological testing
Pediatrician (M.D.)	4-year college degree + 4-year medical degree+ at least three additional years training in pediatrics	Medication management
Psychiatrist, General (M.D.)	4-year college degree + 4-year medical degree+ at least four years training in psychiatry	Children 14 and over, therapy, medication management
Psychiatrist, Child (M.D.)	4-year college degree + 4-year medical degree+ at least five years training in general and child psychiatry	Therapy, medication management

What Can Medication Do?

Medication targets two symptom clusters in "at risk" children. The first symptom cluster involves mood. If your child is depressed, irritable or manic, medication can be very effective in treating the chemical imbalance that underlies the disordered mood. The second symptom cluster involves impulse control. "At risk" children may suffer from such poor impulse control that they cannot respond to discipline. The medication that improves impulse control strengthens inhibition in the brain. Many medications do not produce immediate benefit. It is not unusual for medication to take six to eight weeks or more to work. Ask your doctor about what to expect. Be very careful not to miss doses.

How can you possibly get help in such a system? You have to fight for what you need! Insist on a thorough evaluation by a qualified professional. A child psychologist or psychiatrist is usually the best choice. Assist in the evaluation by providing the evaluator with information. Come to the session with a list of problems and the interventions you have tried. Remember that if nothing you have tried has worked, your child may indeed need medication.

Ideally, decisions regarding medication in children under 14 should be made after consultation with a child psychiatrist. **Medication is most helpful when you also work on changing habits.**

Come to each therapy session with a well-developed set of goals put to paper. Keep a journal on your child's progress and the interventions you have tried. If you keep a daily journal, you will be able to determine whether the treatment is truly effective. Do not try to rely on your memory. One day runs into the next and you cannot possibly remember as well as pencil and paper. Communicate regularly with your child's teachers about his behavior in school.

A therapist talking to your child about his feelings and/or admonishing him to change his behavior has limited value beyond making a diagnosis. Consider this; parents can't help their own children without a solid parent/child relationship. Since relationship is of greatest importance, how can a therapist possibly invest enough time to develop that relationship with your child?

The therapist talking to YOU about your child's behavior and empowering YOU to be a more **responsive** parent is likely to be very helpful. Therefore, expect to be involved in your child's treatment. Do not be surprised or offended if your child's therapist or doctor asks you personal questions. Ask for advice about how to best parent your child. **Realize that your child's needs may be different from those of other children.**

Treatments that involve a therapist forming a bond with your child and using that bond to facilitate change are legitimate. However, insurance companies are increasingly unwilling to pay for the time required for such treatment. It may be bad for your child to form a relationship with a therapist, and then have to break it when the money runs out. Therefore, understand the rationale behind the specific treatment you are getting.

Develop short, medium and long-term goals with your provider. Goals for treatment should center on specific symptoms (see the list below). If you focus on specific symptoms and target behaviors, you will know if your child is benefiting from treatment. The goal of "feeling better" is not specific enough. Your child may say he feels worse or unchanged by treatment you are sure has helped him. If your child fails to improve after three months of treatment, reassess the treatment with your provider. If your child is still unchanged after six months, consider obtaining a second opinion.

10 PROBLEMS REQUIRING PROFESSIONAL EVALUATION

1. Poor impulse control
2. Excessive anger
3. Poor attention span
4. Learning disabilities
5. Oppositional behavior
6. Violent/aggressive behavior
7. Stealing
8. Habitual lying
9. Substance abuse
10. Depression and other mood problems

CHAPTER 12

ON HAVING LOVED A PSYCHOPATH

If you have felt love for someone with antisocial personality disorder, you are not alone. Since these individuals represent up to four per cent of the population, there are a lot of them out there. Each of these individuals has parents, and grandparents, and may also have aunts, uncles, nieces, nephews, cousins, friends, lovers and children. If we guess conservatively that each person with antisocial personality disorder is involved with 5 other people, there are nearly 40 million Americans in the same boat!

This tragedy is discussed over and over again on the nightly news. Tonight, Larry King is on CNN. His guest is the brother of an accused serial killer. This man spoke of the years of Thanksgivings, Christmas Holidays and nights spent playing video games together with his brother, the accused. When asked how he reconciled his relationship with the man accused of killing four people, the guest replied, "My brother isn't a monster like he's portrayed to be." "This is not my brother." The guest just could not let go of the good he saw in his brother even when the evil was painfully obvious.

For me, the thought that 40 million of my fellow Americans are in a similar place, is no real consolation. I still have to answer the question "Why me?" For years, I have warned my patients to be very careful about whom they allow into their lives. Many people develop attachments toward those they spend time with. This time, I wasn't careful enough and didn't follow my own advice. I opened the door to someone who should not have been allowed in. Forgiving myself, after having made such a terrible mistake, is not easy.

What about the more serious issue? Like the brother of the serial killer, I enjoyed the time I spent with a psychopath. I enjoyed our family life, our quiet times and our holidays. I was attached to him and I loved him. On a warm cloudy summer day, my husband and I were out on a rowboat on a lake. He looked at me. I looked at him. He said, "You know, I don't think I've ever loved anyone the way I love you." The moment felt genuine to me, after all I was carrying his child! Yet it wasn't. I thought he was reflecting on our wonderful family (which included my stepson, and two daughters), and on our lives together. For him though, the feelings were shallow. He reported them as part of a plan to con me. And no, I didn't sense the manipulation.

One of the most difficult issues for me to reconcile has been the question of what in my constitution left me vulnerable. Part of my vulnerability lies with these ease with which I love. Through my profession, I have had the great honor of getting to know a large number of people. I have developed deep respect for the human spirit. I found it within myself to like every single one of my patients. To like them I had to find good in them. Finding and appreciating the good in people became a habit– a habit that left me vulnerable to fakers.

I speak of myself here because I do not think I'm that unusual. It is part of human nature to be social and to enjoy each other. I also don't think I want to abandon my love for people, or my optimistic view of others. I hope my children will develop a deep capacity for love. How then, are we all to be protected from those with antisocial personality disorder? The first step is to indeed be selective about who is allowed in. If a mistake is made, corrective action must be taken– even when taking corrective action is very painful. Once I came to really understand my husband for what he is, I resolved to have him out of my life permanently. It was only this step that started the healing process.

Everyone who has shared life with a person with antisocial personality disorder or addiction, should take personal inventory of the experience. I think the most difficult position to be in, is that of mother to an adult with one of these disorders, and grandmother to his/her young child. Often, these grandmothers act as primary caregivers for their grandchildren; since these people are poor parents. Mothers are even more vulnerable than spouses are when it comes to dealing with those with addiction and antisocial personality disorder. Mothers want to believe their offspring are "good" and feel guilt over having raised such a person. They are therefore easily manipulated. Always remember that those with antisocial personality disorder and severe addiction bring evil to most everyone in their lives, including and especially their mothers.

REFERENCES

1. Rhee SH and Waldman ID (2002) Genetic and environmental influences on antisocial behavior: a meta-analysis of Twin and adoption studies *Psychological Bulletin* 128:490-529.

2. Jacobson KE, Prescott CA and Kendle KS (2002) Sex differences in genetic and environmental influences on the development of antisocial behavior *Development and Psychopathology* 14:395-416.

3. Rhee SH and Waldman ID (2002) Genetic and environmental influences on antisocial behavior: a meta-analysis of Twin and adoption studies *Psychological Bulletin* 128:490-529.

Cadoret RJ, Yates, WR Troughton E et. al. (1995) Adoption study demonstrating two genetic pathways to drug abuse *Archives of General Psychiatry* 52:42-52.

4. Rhee SH and Waldman ID (2002) Genetic and environmental influences on antisocial behavior: a meta-analysis of Twin and adoption studies *Psychological Bulletin* 128:490-529.

5. American Psychiatric Association:Diagnostic and Statistical Manuel of Mental Disorders, 4th edition, Text Revision Washington, DC, American Psychiatric Association, 2000.

6. Biederman J, Faraone SV and Monuteaux BA (2002) Differential effect of environmental adversity by gender: Rutter's index of adversity in a grou[p of boys and girls with and without ADHD *American Journal of Psychiatry* 159:607-614.

7. Moss HB, Lynch KG, Hardie TL and Baron DA (2002) Family functioning and peer affiliation in children of fathers with antisocial personality disorder and substance dependence: associations with problem behaviors *American Journal of Psychiatry* 159:607-614.

8. Cloninger CR SigvardssonS and Bohman M (1988) Childhood personality predicts alcohol abuse in young adults Alcohol Clinical and Experimental Research 12:494-504.

Sigvardsson S Bohman M, Cloninger CR (1996) Replication of the Stockholm adoption study of alcoholism: confirmatory cross-fostering analysis *Archives of General Psychiatry* 53:681-687.

Howard MO, Kivlahan D, Walker RD: (1997) Cloniger's tridimensional theory of personality and psychopathology: applications to substance use disorders Journal of Studies in Alcohol 58:48-66.

Cadoret RJ, Yates WR, Troughton E et. al. (1995) Adoption study demonstrating two genetic pathways to drug abuse *Archives of General Psychiatry* 52:42-52.

9. Cloninger CR, Sigvardsson S, and Bohman M (1988) Childhood personality predicts alcohol abuse in young adults Alcohol Clinical and Experimental Research 12:494-504.

Sigvardsson S, Bohman M, Cloninger CR (1996) Replication of the Stockholm adoption study of alcoholism: confirmatory cross-fostering analysis *Archives of General Psychiatry* 53:681-687.

Howard MO, Kivlahan D, Walker RD: (1997) Cloniger's tridimensional theory of personality and psychopathology: applications to substance use disorders Journal of Studies in Alcohol 58:48-66.

10. Cadoret RJ, Yates, WR Troughton E et. al. (1995) Adoption study demonstrating two genetic pathways to drug abuse *Archives of General Psychiatry*52:42-52.

11. Cloninger CR, Sigvardsson S, and Bohman M (1988) Childhood personality predicts alcohol abuse in young adults Alcohol Clinical and Experimental Research 12:494-504.

Sigvardsson S, Bohman M, Cloninger CR (1996) Replication of the Stockholm adoption study of alcoholism: confirmatory cross-fostering analysis *Archives of General Psychiatry* 53:681-687.

Howard MO, Kivlahan D, Walker RD: (1997) Cloniger's tridimensional theory of personality and psychopathology: applications to substance use disorders Journal of Studies in Alcohol 58:48-66.

Cadoret RJ, Yates, WR Troughton E et. al. (1995) Adoption study demonstrating two genetic pathways to drug abuse *Archives of General Psychiatry* 52:42-52.

12. Price TS and Simonoff E et. al. (2005) Continuity and change in preschool ADHD symptoms: longitudinal genetic analysis with contrast effects *Behavioral Genetics* 35:121-132.

13. Faraone SV, Biederman J, Keenan K and Tsuang MT (1991) Separation of DSM III attention deficit disorder and conduct disorder: evidence from a family-genetic study of American child psychiatric patients *Psychological Medicine* 21:109-21.

14. Biederman J, and Farone SV et.al. (1996) Is childhood oppositional defiant disorder a precursor to adolescent conduct disorder? Findings from a four-year follow-up study of children with ADHD *Journal of the American Academy of Child and Adolescent Psychiatry* 35:1193-1204.

15. Biederman J and Mick A et. al. (1996) Influence of gender on attention deficit hyperactivity disorder in children referred to a psychiatric clinic. *American Journal of Psychiatry* 159:36-42.

16. Biederman J, Farone SV and Keenan K et.al. (1992) Further evidence for family-genetic risk factors in ADHD: Patterns of Comorbidity in probands and relatives of psychiatrically and pediatrically referred samples. *Archives of General Psychiatry* 49:728-738.

17. American Psychiatric Association:Diagnostic and Statistical Manuel of Mental Disorders, 4ᵗʰ edition, Text Revision, Washington, DC, American Psychiatric Association, 2000.

18. Hare RD (1993) *Without Conscience* The Guilford Press, New York, NY

19. Frick PJ and Morris AS (2004) Temperament and developmental pathways to conduct problems. *Journal of Clinical Child and Adolescent Psychology* 33:54-68.

20. Raine A (2002) Annotation: The role of prefrontal deficits, low autonomic arousal, and early health factors in the development of antisocial and aggressive behavior in children. *Journal of Child Psychology and Psychiatry* 43:417-434.

Ogloff J and Wong S (1990) Electrodermal and cardiovascular evidence of a coping response in psychopaths. *Criminal Justice and Behavior* 17:231-45.

21. Blonigen DM, and Hicks BM et.al. (2005) Psychopathic Personality traits: heritability and genetic overlap with internalizing and externalizing psychopathology

Psychological Medicine 35:637-648

22. Kandel ER, SchwartzJH, Jessell T (1991) *Principles of Neuroscience* Elsevier Press, New York, NY.

23. Bowlby J The nature of a child's tie to his mother *International Journal of Psychoanalysis* (1958) 39:350-373.

24. Ainsworth MDS, Blehar MC, Waters E and Wall J (1978) *Patterns of Attachment: A psychological study of the strange situation.* Erlbaum, Hillsdale, NJ.

25. Raine A (2002) Annotation: The role of prefrontal deficits, low autonomic arousal, and early health factors in the development of antisocial and aggressive behavior in children *Journal of Child Psychology and Psychiatry* 43:417-434.

26. Lickona T (1981) *Raising good children* Bantam Books, New York, NY.

27. Wakschlag LS and Hans SL (2002) Maternal smoking during pregnancy and conduct problems in high risk youth: a developmental framework Developmental Psychopathology 14:351-369.

28. Smyke AT, Boris NW and Alexander GM (2002) Fear of Spoiling in at-risk African American mothers Child Psychiatry and Human Development 32:295-30 (I found this reference after I wrote this paragraph, I never personally observed fear of spoiling in African American mothers. Fear of spoiling is found in many different groups.)

29. Trainor LJ (2005) Are there critical periods for musical development? *Developmental Psychobiology* 46:262-278.

30. Kochanska G and Murray KT (2000) Mother-child mutually responsive orientation and conscience development: from toddler to early school age *Child Development* 71:417-431

31. Kazdin AE, Whitley MK (2003) Treatment of parental stress to enhance therapeutic change among children referred for aggressive and antisocial behavior. *Journal of Consulting Clinical Psychology* 71:504-515.

32. Kochanska G and Aksan N (2004) Links between systems of inhibition from infancy to preschool years *Child Development* 75:1477-1490. Olson SL, Bates JE and Bayles K (1990) Early antecedents of childhood impulsivity: the role of parent-child interaction, cognitive competence, and temperament *Journal of Abnormal Child Psychology* 18:317-334.

33. Kochanska, G and Askan N (2004) Development of mutual responsiveness between parents and their young children. *Child Development* 75:1657-1676:

34. Wigal SB, Nemet D, Swanson JM (2003) Catecholamine response to exercise in children with attention deficit hyperactivity disorder (2003) *Pediatric Research* 53:756-761.

35. Keller H, and Yovsi R et. al. (2004) Developmental Consequences of Early parenting experiences Self-Recognition and Self Regulation in three cultural communities. *Child Development* 75:1745-1760:

36. Decety J and Jackson PL (2004) The functional architecture of human empathy *Behavioral and Cognitive Neuroscience Reviews* 3:71-100

37. Valiente C, Eisenberg N, Fabes RA et.al. (2004) Prediction of children's empathy-related responding from their effortful control and parent's expressivity*Developmental Psychology* 40:911-926.

38. Children's distress is universally related to parent's negativity, see article above.

39. Bellisle F, McDevitt R, Prentice AM (1997) Meal frequency and energy balance *British Journal of Nutrition* 77Suppl 1:S57-S70.

40. Ainsworth MDS and Bell SM (1969) Some contemporary patterns of mother-infant interaction in the feeding situation in *Stimulation in Early Infancy*, Academic Press New York, NY

41. Harlow HF (1971) *Learning to Love* Albion Publishing Company, San Francisco, CA

42. Dishion TJ and Patterson SG (1996) *Preventive parenting with love encouragement and limits* Castalia Publishing Company, Eugene, OR.

43. Frick PJ and Morris AS (2004) Temperament and developmental pathways to conduct problems Journal of Clinical Child and Adolescent Psychology 33:54-68.

44. Decety J and Jackson PL (2004) The functional architecture of human empathy *Behavioral and Cognitive Neuroscience Reviews* 3:71-100
Valiente C, Eisenberg N, Fabes RA et.al. (2004) Prediction of children's empathy-related responding from their effortful control and parent's expressivity *Developmental Psychology* 40:911-926.

45. Antshel K and Remer R (2003) Social skills training in children with attention deficit hyperactivity disorder: a randomized clinical trial *Journal of Clinical child and adolescent psychology* 32:153-165.
Valiente C, Eisenberg N, Fabes RA et.al. (2004) Prediction of children's empathy-related responding from their effortful control and parent's expressivity*Developmental Psychology* 40:911-926.

46. Laible DJ, and Thompson RA (2000) Mother-child discourse, attachment security, shared positive affect, and early conscience development. *Child Development* 71:1424-1440.
Laible DJ, and Thompson RA (2002) Mother-child conflict in the toddler years: lessons in emotion, morality, and relationships *Child Development* 73:1187-1203.
Laible DJ, and Thompson RA (1998) Attachment and emotional understanding in preschool children *Developmental Psychology* 34:1038-1045.
Laible DJ (2004) Mother-child discourse in two contexts: links with child temperament, attachment security, and socioemotional competence *Developmental Psychology* 40:979-992.

47. Dyck MJ, Farrugia C, Sochet IM and Holmes-Brown M (2004) Emotion recognition/understanding ability in hearing or vision-impaired children: do sounds, sights or words make the difference? *Journal of Child Psychology and Psychiatry* 45:789-800.

48. Braaten EB and Rosen LA (2000) Self regulation of affect in attention deficit-hyperactivity disorder (ADHD) and non-ADHD boys: differences in empathetic responding *Journal of Consulting and Clinical Psychology* 68:313-321.

49. Blair RJ, Colledge E Murray L and Mitchell DG (2001) A selective impairment in the processing of sad and fearful facial expressions in children with psychopathic tendencies *Journal of Abnormal Child Psychology* 29:491-498.

50. Krevans J and Gibbs JC (1996) Parents use of inductive discipline: relations to children's empathy and prosocial behavior Child Development. 67:3263-3277.

51. Rodkin PC, Farmer TW, Pearl R, Van Acker R (2000) Heterogeneity of popular boys: antisocial and prosocial configurations 36:14-24.

52. Funk JB (2005) Children's exposure to violent video games and desensitization to violence *Child and Adolescent Psychiatric Clinics of North America* 14:387-404.

53. Moss HB, Lynch KG, Hardie TL and Baron DA (2002) Family functioning and peer affiliation in children of fathers with antisocial personality disorder and substance dependence: associations with problem behaviors *American Journal of Psychiatry* 159:607-614.

54. Sroufe LA, Carlson EA, Levy AK and Egeland B (1999) Implications of attachment theory for developmental psychopathology *Developmental psychopathology* 11:1-13.

55. Lee AL, Ogle WO and Sapolsky RM (2002) Stress and depression: possible links to neuron cell death in the hippocampus *Bipolar Disorder* 4:117-128.

56. Wyman PA, Cowan EL Work WC et. al. (1992) Interviews with children who experienced major life stress: family and child attributes that predict resilient outcomes *Journal of the American Academy of Child and Adolescent Psychiatry* 31:904-910.

57. Gunnar MR (1998) Quality of early care and buffering of neuroendocrine stress reactions: potential effects on the developing human brain *Preventive Medicine* 27:208-211.

58. Kochanska, G and Askan N (2004) Development of mutual responsiveness between parents and their young children. *Child Development* 75:1657-1676:

59. Jaffe SR, Moffitt TE, Caspi A (2003) Life with (or without) father: the benefits of living with two biological parents depend on the father's antisocial behavior *Child Development* 74:109-126.

60. Moeller GF, Barratt ES, Dougherty DM et. al. (2001) Psychiatric aspects of impulsivity *American Journal of Psychiatry* 158:1783-1793.

61. Raine A (2002) Annotation: The role of prefrontal deficits, low autonomic arousal, and early health factors in the development of antisocial and aggressive behavior in children *Journal of Child Psychology and Psychiatry* 43:417-434.

62. MacKenzie RJ (2001) *Setting limits with your strong willed child* Three Rivers Press, New York, NY.

63. Proverbs 22:6, New American Standard Translation

64. Dishion TJ and Patterson SG (1996) *Preventive parenting with love encouragement and limits* Castalia Publishing Company, Eugene, OR.

65. Holden GW and West MJ (1989) Proximate regulation by mothers: a demonstration of how differing styles affect young children's behavior *Child Development* 60:64-69.

Frankel KA and Bates JE (1990) Mother-toddler problem solving: antecedents in attachment, home behavior, and temperament *Child Development* 61:810-819.

66. Dishion TJ and Patterson SG (1996) *Preventive parenting with love encouragement and limits* Castalia Publishing Company, Eugene, OR.

Schaefer CE. and DiGeronimo TF *Teach Your Child to Behave* (1991) Penguin Books, New York, NY

MacKenzie RJ (2001) *Setting limits with your strong willed child* Three Rivers Press, New York, NY.

67. MacKenzie RJ (2001) *Setting limits with your strong willed child* Three Rivers Press, New York, NY.

68. Nigg JT, Hill Goldsmith H and Sachek J (2004) Temperament and attention deficit hyperactivity disorder: The development of a multiple pathway model *Journal of Clinical Child and Adolescent Psychology* 33:42-53.

Olsen SL, Schilling EM and Bates JE (1999) Measurement of impulsivity: construct coherence, longitudinal stability, and relationship with externalizing problems in middle childhood and adolescence.

Cloninger CR Sigvardsson S and Bohman M (1988) Childhood personality predicts alcohol abuse in young adults Alcohol Clinical and Experimental Research 12:494-504.

Sigvardsson S Bohman M, Cloninger CR (1996) Replication of the Stockholm adoption study of alcoholism: confirmatory cross-fostering analysis *Archives of General Psychiatry* 53:681-687.

Howard MO, Kivlahan D, Walker RD: Cloniger's tridimensional theory of personality and psychopathology: applications to substance use disorders (1997) Journal of Studies in Alcohol 58:48-66.

Cadoret RJ, Yates, WR Troughton E et. al. (1995) Adoption study demonstrating two genetic pathways to drug abuse *Archives of General Psychiatry* 52:42-52.

69. Nigg JT, Hill Goldsmith H and Sachek J (2004) Temperament and attention deficit hyperactivity disorder: The development of a multiple pathway model *Journal of Clinical Child and Adolescent Psychology* 33:42-53.

70. Valiente C, Eisenberg N, Fabes RA et.al. (2004) Prediction of children's empathy-related responding from their effortful control and parent's expressivity *Developmental Psychology* 40:911-926.

71. Shapiro, LE (1997) *How to raise a child with a high EQ* HarperCollins Publishers Inc., New York, NY.

Wilde J (1997) *Hot stuff to help kids chill out* LGR Publishing, Richmond, IN.

72. Nippold MA Duthrie JK and Larsen J (2005) Literacy as a leisure activity: free-time preferences of older children and young adolescents *Language Speech Hearing Services in Schools* 36:93-102.

73. Shahin A, Roberts LE and Trainor LJ (2004) Enhancement of auditory cortical development by musical experience in children. *Neuroreports* 15:1917-1921.

74. Jackson NA (2003) A survey of music therapy methods and their role in the treatment of early elementary school children with ADHD *Journal of Music Therapy* 40:302-323.

75. Rauscher FH, Shaw GL and Levine LJ et. al. (1997) Music training causes long-term enhancement of prescholl children's spatial-temporal reasoning.Neurology Research 19:2-8.

76. Cheek JM and Smith LR (1999) Music training and mathematics achievement *Adolescence* 34:759-761.

77. Kochanska G and Knaak A (2003) Effortful control as a personality characteristic of young children: antecedents, correlates, and consequences *Journal of Personality* 71:1087-1112.

78. Fowles DC, and Kochanska G (2000) Temperament as a moderator of pathways to conscience in children: the contribution of electrodermal activity. *Psychophysiology*

37:788-795.

79. Kochanska G, Gross JN, Lin MH and Nicholes KE (2002) Guilt in young children: development, determinants, and relations with a broader system of standards *Child Development* 73:461-482

80. Rowe R, Maughan B, Worthman CM et. al. (2004) Testosterone, antisocial behavior, and social dominance in boys: pubertal development and biosocial interaction *Biologic Psychiatry* 55: 546-552.

81. Blair RJR (2001) Neurocognitive models of aggression, the antisocial personality disorders, and psychopathy Journal of Neurology Neurosurgery and Psychiatry 71: 727-731

82. Taylor ER, Kelly J, Valescu S, et.al. Is stealing a gateway crime? (2005) *Psychological Medicine* 35: 163-174.

Anderson CA, Hinshaw SP and Simmel C Mother-child interactions in ADHD and comparison boys: relationships with overt and covert externalizing behavior (1994) *Journal of Abnormal Child Psychology* 22:247-265.

83. Loeber R, Stouthamer-Loeber G and Green SM (1991) Age at onset of problem behavior in boys, and later disruptive and delinquent behaviors. Criminal Behavior and Mental Health 1:229-246.

84. Dilsaver SC, Henderson-Fuller S and Akiskal HS (2003) Occult mood disorders in 104 consequtively presenting children referred for the treatemtn of attention-deficit/hyperactivity disorder in a community mental health clinic *Journal of Clinical Psychiatry* 64:1170-1176.

85. Kohlberg, L (1991) The *Meaning and Measurement of Moral Development.* Clark University Press, Worchester, MA

86. Birbaumer N, Veit R and Lotze M et. Al. (2005) Deficient fear conditioning in psychopathy *Archives of General Psychiatry* 62:799-805.

87a. Freedman JS (1965) Warning, Distraction and Resistance to Influence *Journal of Personality and Social Psychology* 1:262-266.

87b. Kochanska G Aksan N and Nicholes KE (2003) Maternal power assertion in discipline and moral discourse contexts: commonalities, differences, and implications for children's moral conduct and cognition *Developmental Psychology* 39:949-963.

Foreman DR and Kochanska G (2001) Viewing imitation as child responsiveness: a link between teaching and discipline domains of socialization *Developmental Psychology* 37:198-206.

Kochanska G, Forman DR Aksan N and Dunbar DR (2005) Pathways to conscience: early mother-child mutually responsive orientation and children's moral emotion, conduct and cognition *Journal of Child Psychology and Psychiatry* 46:19-34.

Kochanska G, Aksan N, and Carlson J (2005) Temperament, relationships, and young children's receptive cooperation with their parents *Developmental Psychology in press.*

Cunningham CE and Boyle MH (2002) Preschoolers at risk for attention-deficit hyperactivity disorder and oppositional defiant disorder: family, parenting and behavioral correlates *Journal of abnormal child psychology* 30:555-569.

88. Rowe R and Maughan Bet. Al. (2004) Testosterone, antisocial behavior, and social dominance in boys: pubertal development and biosocial interaction. *Biological Psychiatry*

55:546-552.

89. Keller H and Yovsi R et.al. (2004) Developmental consequences of early parenting experiences: Self-recognition and Self-Regulation in three cultural communities *Child Development* 75:1745-1760.

90. Kochanska G, Forman DR, Aksan N and Dunbar DR (2005) Pathways to conscience: early mother-child mutually responsive orientation and children's moral emotion, conduct and cognition *Journal of Child Psychology and Psychiatry* 46:19-34.

91. Laible DJ, and Thompson RA (2000) Mother-child discourse, attachment security, shared positive affect, and early conscience development. *Child Development* 71:1424-1440.

92. Holden GW and West MJ (1989) Proximate regulation by mothers: a demonstration of how differing styles affect young children's behavior *Child Development* 60:64-69.

93. Silverman IW and Ragusa DM (1992) A short-term longitudinal study of the early development of self-regulation *Journal of Abnormal Child Psychology* 20:415-435.

Olsen SL, Bates JE and Bayles K (1990) Early antecedents of childhood impulsivity: the role of parent-child interaction, cognitive competence, and temperament *Journal of Abnormal Child Psychology* 18:317-334.

94. Sroufe LA, Carlson EA, Levy AK and Egeland B (1999) Implications of attachment theory for developmental psychopathology *Developmental psychopathology* 11:1-13.

95. Cloninger CR SigvardssonS and Bohman M (1988) Childhood personality predicts alcohol abuse in young adults. *Alcohol Clinical and Experimental Research* 12:494-504.

Brunelle C, Assaad JM and Barrett SP et.al. (2004) Heightened heart rate response to alcohol intoxication is associated with a reward-seeking personality profile *Alcohol Clinical and Experimental Research* 28:394-401.

96. Beechara A (2003) Risky business: emotion, decision-making, and addiction *Journal of Gambling Studies* 19:23-51.

97. Beechara A, Damasio H (2002) Decision-making and addiction (part I): impaired activation of somatic states in substance dependent individuals when pondering decisions with negative future consequences *Neuropsychologia* 40:1675-1689.

Beechara A, Dolan S and Hindes A (2002) Decision-making and addiction (part II): myopia for the future or hypersensitivity to reward *Neuropsychologia* 40:1690-1705.

98. Myers MG, Stewart DG and Brown SA (1998) Progression from conduct disorder to antisocial personality disorder following treatment for adolescent substance abuse *American Journal of Psychiatry* 155:479-485.

99. Myers MG, Stewart DG and Brown SA (1998) Progression from conduct disorder to antisocial personality disorder following treatment for adolescent substance abuse *American Journal of Psychiatry* 155:479-485.

100. Iocono WG, Malone SM and McGue M (2003) Substance use disorders, externalizing psychopathology, and P300 event-related potential amplitude *International Journal of Psychophysiology* 48:147-178.

101. Milberger S, Biederman J Faraone SV and Jones J (1998) Further evidence of an association between maternal smoking during pregnancy and attention deficit

hyperactivity disorder: findings from a high-risk sample of siblings *Journal of Clinical Child Psychology* 27:352-358.

102. Biederman J, Faraone SV and Monuteaux MC (2002) Differential effect of environmental adversity by gender: Rutter's index of adversity in a group of boys and girls with and without ADHD.*American Journal of Psychiatry* 159:1556-1562.

103. Biederman J and Faraone SV (2004) The Massachusetts General Hospital studies of gender influences on attention deficit hyperactivity/disorder in youths and relatives *Psychiatric Clinics of North America* 27:225-232.

104. Faraone SV and Biederman J et.al. (2000) Family study of girls with attention deficit hyperactivity disorder *American Journal of Psychiatry* 157:1077-1083.

Neuman R and Todd R et.al. (1999) Evaluation of ADHD topology in three contrasting samples: a latent class approach. *Journal of the American Academy of Child and Adolescent Psychiatry* 38:25-33.

Hudziak J and Heath A et.al. (1998) Latent class and factor analysis of DSM IV ADHD: a twin study of female adolescents *Journal of the American Academy of Child and Adolescent Psychiatry* 37:848-857.

Sherman D, Iacono W and McGue M (1997) Attention deficit hyperactivity disorder dimensions: a twin study of inattention and impulsivity hyperactivity *Journal of the American Academy of Child and Adolescent Psychiatry* 36:745-753.

105. Slaats-Willemse D, Swaab-Barneveld H, De Sonneville L and Buitelaar J (2005) Familial clustering of executive functionsing in affected sibling pair families with ADHD *Journal of the American Academy of Child and Adolescent Psychiatry* 44"385-391

106. Price TS and Siminoff E et.al. (2005) Continuity and change in preschool ADHD symptoms:longitudinal genetic analysis with contrast effects *Behavioral Genetics* 35:121-132.

107. MTA Cooperative Group A 14-month randomized clinical trial of treatment strategies for attention-deficit/hyperactivity disorder. The MTA Cooperative Group. Multimodal treatment study of children with ADHD *Archives of General Psychiatry* 56:1073-1086

108. Matthys W, Cuperus JM and Van Engeland H (1999) Deficient social problem-solving in boys with ODD/CD, with ADHD and with both disorders.*Journal of the American Academy of Child and Adolescent Psychiatry* 3:311-321.8

109. Walcott CM and Landau S (2004) The relation between disinhibition and emotion regulation in boys with attention deficit hyperactivity disorder. *Journal of Child and Adolescent Psychology* 33:772-782.

110. Biederman J and Faraone SV (2004) The Massachusetts General Hospital studies of gender influences on attention deficit hyperactivity/disorder in youths and relatives *Psychiatric Clinics of North America* 27:225-232.

111. Flory K and Milich R et.al. (2003) Relation between childhood disruptive behavior disorders and substance use and dependence symptoms in young adulthood: individuals with symptoms of attention-deficit/hyperactivity disorder and conduct disorder are uniquely at risk.*Psychology of Addictive Behavior* 17:151-158.

112. Barkley RA, Fischer M, Smallish MA and Fletcher K (2003) Does the treatment of Attention deficit/hyperactivity disorder with stimulants contribute to drug use/abuse? A 13-year prospective study *Pediatrics* 111:97-109.

113. Biederman J and Mick A et. al. Influence of gender on attention deficit hyperactivity disorder in children referred to a psychiatric clinic *American Journal of Psychiatry* 159:36-42.

114. Faraone SV, and Biederman J et.al. (1998) Familial subtypes of attention deficit hyperactivity disorder: a 4-year follow-up study of children from antisocial-ADHD families *Journal of Child Psychology and Psychiatry* 39:1045-1053.

115. Herpertz SC and Wenning B et.al. (2001) Psychophysiological responses in ADHD boys with and without conduct disorder: implications for adult antisocial behavior Journal of the American Academy of Child and Adolescent Psychiatry 40:1222-1230.

116. Barkley RA, Fischer M, Smallish L and Fletcher K (2004) Young adult follow-up of hyperactive children: antisocial activities and drug use.*Journal of Child Psychology and Psychiatry* 45:195-211.

117. Speltz ML, Coy K and DeKlyen M et. al. (1998) Early-onset oppositional defiant disorder: what factors predict it's course? *Seminars in Clinical Neuropsychiatry* 3:302-319.

118. Kerr DC, Lopez NL, Olson SL and Sameroff AJ (2004) Parental discipline and externalizing behavior problems in early childhood: the roles of moral regulation and child gender *Abnormal Child Psychology* 32:369-383.

119. MacKenzie RJ (2001) *Setting limits with your strong willed child* Three Rivers Press, New York, NY.

120. Kiang L , Moreno AJ and Robinson JL (2004) Maternal Preconceptions about parenting predict child temperament, maternal sensitivity and children's empathy. *Developmental Psychology* 40:1081-1092.

121. Lickona T (1981) *Raising good children* Bantam Books, New York, NY

122. Ephesians 6:4, New American Standard Translation

123. Van den Boom DC (1994) The influence of temperament and mothering on attachment and exploration: An experimental manipulation of sensitive responsiveness among lower class mothers of irritable infants *Child Development 65:1457-1477.*

124. Strand PS (2002) Coordination of maternal directives with preschoolers' behavior: Influence of maternal coordination training on dyadic activity and child compliance *Journal of Clinical Child and Adolescent Psychology* 31:6-15.

125. Olds D, Henderson CR, Cole R et.al. (1998) Long-term effects of nurse home visitation on children's criminal and antisocial behavior: 15 year follow-up of a randomized controlled trial *JAMA* 280:1238-1244.

126. Reid MJ Webster-Stratton C and Baydar N (2004) Halting the development of conduct problems in head start children: the effects of parent training *Journal of Clinical Child and Adolescent Psychology* 33:279-291.

127. Dishion TJ A family-Centered approach to the prevention of early-onset antisocial behavior: two-year effects of the family checkup in early childhood- *personal communication.*

128. Ryan RM and Deci EL (2001) On happiness and human potentials: A review of research on hedonic and eudaimonic well-being *Annual Reviews of Psychology* 52:141-166.

129. The use of authority to combat bullying is also advocated by other authors. See Lickona T (1981) *Raising good children* Bantam Books, New York, NY, page 145-146.

INDEX

Looking for help parenting your at risk child?

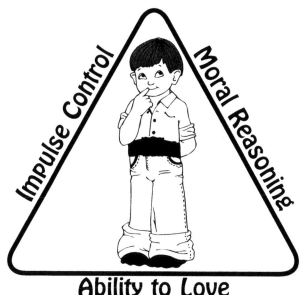

Ability to Love

PARENTINGTHEATRISKCHILD.COM

- ♥ At this site you will find a workbook to accompany this book.
- ♥ An online community of parents who are raising at risk kids.
- ♥ Resources to help your child succeed in school and in life.
- ♥ Email Dr. Leedom: ljleedom@parentingtheatriskchild.com,
- ♥ Send us your own stories.
- ♥ Give us feedback about this book.